Praise for *The Taste of Joy*

"It is a pleasure to team up with Emily, as we share a similar passion for food, especially as we navigate Mediterranean cuisine. We share the belief that eating seasonally and from locally sourced ingredients is a more responsible way to approach a higher quality of life."

—Ariel Guivisdalsky, professional chef, instructor, and columnist of "A Chef and a Foodie on Tour"

"It has been amazing to see Emily immerse herself in local traditions and embrace all that is Maltese. This book reminds us that life is meant to be relished and not just endured."

—Matthew Towns, international professional football goalkeeper and coach

"We love having Emily on our TV show *Hygieia*! Her enthusiasm, her passion, and of course her knowledge are an inspiration to all the viewers!"

—Marika Caruana Smith, host of *Hygieia with Marika* on Malta TVM

"We came to Malta to film the Maltese specialty foods. Naturally, we had to do an episode on the famous Maltese pastizzi with Emily as our guide! What Emily brings to the table is her enthusiasm and passion for all things Malta and Mediterranean living. This book brings that excitement to you in the way only Emily can."

—Giulia Ottaviano, TV producer and director

"Emily A. Francis has written a must-read book for anyone considering starting a healthier life full of joy with a little bit of extra spice! Read this delightful guide full of lessons to nourish not only your mind and soul but also your body with additional easy recipes and food tips and learn to love and live the Mediterranean way of life."

—Elena & Melisa Koyunseven, founders of *The Mediterranean Lifestyle* magazine

"Malta has been Emily's home for the past few years. At *Oh My Malta*, she indulges her passion for the Maltese Islands and the Mediterranean by enthusiastically sharing her knowledge of local produce and cuisine in the most fascinating of ways with visitors and locals alike, radiating positive energy wherever she goes and reminding us all why we love Malta and Mediterranean living so much. It's a true pleasure having her on our team! We know you will love this book!"

—Philippa Zammit, editor at *Oh My Malta* magazine

the
TASTE
of
JOY

© Jade Attard

About the Author

Emily A. Francis has a BS in exercise science and wellness with a minor in nutrition and a master's degree in human performance. She is the host of the show *All About Healing* on Healthy Life Radio and the author of *Stretch Therapy, The Body Heals Itself, Whole Body Healing,* and *Healing Ourselves Whole.* With her move to the Mediterranean, she has become fascinated with local food production, writing a regular column in the local tourism magazine *Oh My Malta* titled "Emily in Malta," where she interviews local farmers, fishermen, and chefs on single ingredient farming. She has also teamed up with Chef Ariel Guivisdalsky for a food review column called "A Chef and a Foodie on Tour." She is a contributing writer for Malta's *Gourmet Today* magazine.

You can find Emily at MyMaltaLife.com. Click the tab "Emily in Malta" to check out the video interviews and put a name to the face of each farmer and fisherman mentioned in the book! She can also be found on social media and at EmilyAFrancisBooks.com.

the
TASTE
of
JOY

Mediterranean Wisdom
for a Life Worth Savoring

Author of *The Body Heals Itself*

EMILY A. FRANCIS

Llewellyn Publications • Woodbury, Minnesota

FIRST EDITION
First Printing, 2023

Cover design by Kevin R. Brown

Llewellyn Publications is a registered trademark of Llewellyn Worldwide Ltd.

Library of Congress Cataloging-in-Publication Data

Names: Francis, Emily A., author.
Title: The taste of joy : Mediterranean wisdom for a life worth savoring /
    Emily A. Francis.
Description: First edition. | Woodbury, Minnesota : Llewellyn Worldwide,
    [2022] | Includes bibliographical references. | Summary: "*The Taste of
    Joy* shows you the value of living simply, mindfully, seasonally, and
    naturally, while feeding the body and soul more richly. Explore your own
    path to happiness as Emily recounts her eye-opening experiences getting
    to know a new region, its inhabitants, and their culture. With Emily's
    thought-provoking pearls of wisdom and a handful of recipes, you can get
    a taste of blissful happiness and discover how to create a quality life
    you can relish instead of simply endure"— Provided by publisher.
Identifiers: LCCN 2022036865 (print) | LCCN 2022036866 (ebook) | ISBN
    9780738773681 (paperback) | ISBN 9780738773872 (ebook)
Subjects: LCSH: Cooking, Mediterranean. | Contentment. | Self-realization.
    | Life change events. | Francis, Emily A.—Homes and haunts. | LCGFT:
    Cookbooks.
Classification: LCC TX725.M35 F73 2022 (print) | LCC TX725.M35 (ebook) |
    DDC 641.59/1822—dc23/eng/20220810
LC record available at https://lccn.loc.gov/2022036865
LC ebook record available at https://lccn.loc.gov/2022036866

Llewellyn Worldwide Ltd. does not participate in, endorse, or have any authority or responsibility concerning private business transactions between our authors and the public.

All mail addressed to the author is forwarded but the publisher cannot, unless specifically instructed by the author, give out an address or phone number.

Any internet references contained in this work are current at publication time, but the publisher cannot guarantee that a specific location will continue to be maintained. Please refer to the publisher's website for links to authors' websites and other sources.

Llewellyn Publications
A Division of Llewellyn Worldwide Ltd.
2143 Woodiale Drive
Woodbury, MN 55125-2989
www.llewellyn.com

Printed in the United States of America

Other Books by Emily A. Francis

Healing Ourselves Whole
(Health Communications, 2021)

Whole Body Healing
(Llewellyn, 2020)

The Body Heals Itself
(Llewellyn, 2017)

Stretch Therapy
(Blue River Press, 2013)

Acknowledgments

I extend my deepest gratitude to the Pace family. To the mother and father, sisters, and brother who built a house made from limestone and love for their family…and mine. Thank you for opening your hearts and home to us. I am so very thankful it was you.

Thank you to my greatest loves: Scott, Hannah, Ava, Christopher, Nicholas, Mom, Gretchen, Bradley and Marina, James, Jan and Chuck, and all our family and friends back home: You are my everything and I thank God, the moon, the sun, the sea, and all my lucky stars for each of you every day. Thank you for supporting us so strongly that we could do something so daring as to move halfway across the world and truly appreciate and enjoy ourselves in our new adventure. That is so much more easily done with the support we know we have from each of you.

Thank you to my ladies in Malta: Doreen, Michelle, Juliana, and Elena, for being my best friends who became my family.

To everyone who made this book possible: There are a lot of people who made each story possible. I will list their names in no particular order: Thank you to Gareth and Barbara Genner for making this incredible life possible. Thanks also to the Gowasack family and the Valdes family. Thank you to the Parkers: Doreen, Paul, and TJ; the entire Pace family; the Abela family: Michelle, Eli, and Gerald; the Cortes family: Juliana, Arthur, Eric, and Alice; and the Tsarev family: Mikhail, Elena, Alexandr, Elina, and Misha. Jade Attard, Amy Micallef Decesare, James Bianchi, Philippa Zammit, Fabrizio Oliva, Paul Zammit, Josephine Xuereb, and the Cini family, Aaron Camilleri, Sam Cremona, Dermott Sales, Salvatore Romano, Ariel Guivisdalsky, Loukia Makou and the Panagiotopoulos family, Marc and Stéphanie Frasson-Botton and family, Brian Camilleri and family, Natasha Gafa, Andre Grech, Venunzio Gafa and family, and Matthew Towns. The Farrugias: Heathcliff, Ruby, and family; the Camilleri family: Dane, Vanessa, and family. Thank you, Tony and Irene Borg, Gordon Calleja, George Attard, Joseph DeBrincat, Joseph Muscat, Marion Cini, René and Johanna Van Lent, April DeLac, David Attard, Sandeep and Melissa Virk, Marika Caruana Smith, Ben Muscat and family, Giulia

Ottaviano, Jennie Rose and Norman Fernando, Svetlana Muscat, Ronald Bugeja, Jan Little, Jennifer Dollander, Jennie Lee, Michelle Cefai, Neil Hitchcock, Gloria Camilleri, Pawlu Debono, Daniel Pisani, Larken Bugeja, Elena and Melisa Koyunseven, Hon. Clayton Bartolo MP, Minister for Tourism in Malta, Joseph Bartolo, Ayrton Mifsud, Kurt Mifsud, David Vella, Rodney Gauci, Elton Zarb, Aldo Spiteri, and Jane Borg. (If I left out any names, my sincere apologies.)

A special thank you: Angela Wix and Andrea Neff, my incredible editors, for making this book clean up so shiny and bright! Thank you, Kat Neff, Marianne Pestana, and Jade Attard for publicity that I desperately need! There is nothing like being part of such an amazing team!

Thank you so much: Steve Harris, my Literary Agent Extraordinaire. You are the very best there is!

Thank you to these farms and services:
Malta Tourism Ministry
Mediterranean Culinary Academy
Mediterranean Olive Oil Academy
Mellieha Homemade Jam
Malta Sunripe
Xwejni Salt Pans by Leli tal-Melh
Karwija Farm
Wardija Extra Virgin Olive Oils/Ghajn Rasul Co. Ltd.
Ta' Salut Farms
Ġbejniet tal-Kejken
ROMAN Fresh Fish
Popeye Farmers
Ta' Marija Restaurant
Corradino Correctional Bakery
Vincent's Eco Estate
Malta Chocolate Factory
Bureau Vallée Malta
WickedandLoud Malta
Grima Family Olive Oil Orchard

I fondly dedicate this book to my beloved Malta.
Thank you for loving us so well.
Grazzi minn qalbi! (Thank you from the bottom of my heart!)

Here's to our beautiful and delicious life,
tasting the joy in every bite.
Mela!

Contents: The Menu

Recipes

This book uses food and recipes as metaphors for life. While this is not a cookbook, each chapter does include simple recipes for you to make to engage more deeply with each metaphor. I wanted to include recipes that I have picked up from living in the Mediterranean to better introduce you to the pure and simple approach to both food and life here.

"Try not to resist the changes that come your way.
Instead, let life live through you.
And do not worry that your life is turning upside down.
How do you know that the side you are used to
is better than the one to come?"
—Rumi

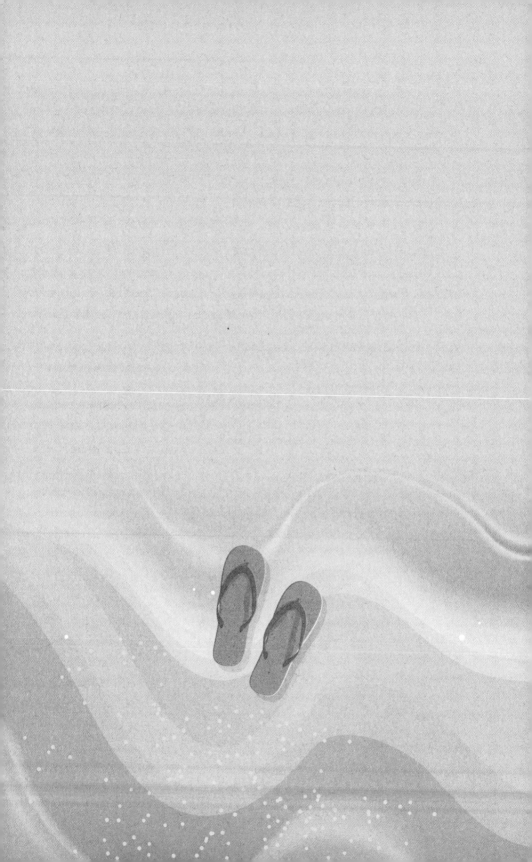

Foreword

Welcome to Malta! A cliché? Not quite. Malta is a country, but it is so much more than a small dot on the map. My welcome is to our natural beauty, our blue and shimmering Mediterranean Sea, our 300 days of sunshine, our 7,000 years of history, our cuisine, our ancient towns and villages, our colourful culture and cosmopolitan lifestyle, and our warm hospitality.

Visiting us is not just about discovering a small archipelago smack in the middle of the Mediterranean. The experience is more akin to gently peeling one fascinating layer of reality after another. By the time you get to the core, you'll be hooked. For life. This is what I welcome you to.

As the dark days of the pandemic slowly ebb away, tourism is steadily coming back into its own. From the confines of their living rooms, families, men, women, and children are heading to destinations near and far.

According to the World Tourism Organization, in the first five months of 2022 the sector has bounced back to 46% of what it was just before the pandemic hit in 2019. The news is even better for Malta. By June of this year, our tourism sector was already back to 74% of where it was in the pre-pandemic days. This performance is comparable to that of some of the top and much larger destinations in our region, like Spain and Portugal. Not bad at all.

How is this resilience, this exceptionally rapid recovery, to be explained? Sure, as mentioned above, we have been blessed on all fronts as far as the cornerstones of tourism are concerned. But today's travelling hinges on memorable experiences. Essentially, in terms of policy, success is all about constantly and smartly curating our tourism offer. It is also about anticipating the new trends coming up on the horizon. This is what explains our rapid resilience.

Accordingly, as a government we have worked hard on a two-pronged tourism strategy, focusing on making our offer sustainable on all counts while simultaneously ensuring that we deliver quality experiences. It is on these two pillars that we are building the future we envision.

As tourism minister, I believe that we should always dream beyond what we have already achieved, beyond what we are already offering. Staying put is not in the cards for us. At the same time, however, we dream with both feet firmly planted on the ground. Aiming high is pointless unless one maintains a solid grip on the economic, political, and social realities shaping the future at home and abroad. In this sense, we are acutely conscious of the direct and indirect consequences of the pandemic and military conflicts around the world on tourism. We cannot choose to ignore them.

Yet the formidable challenges that lie ahead should temper our optimism, not extinguish it. Our realism should continue to drive us to turn these challenges into opportunities. As we are emerging out of a few unprecedented years, our tourism vision needs to be strengthened and clarified by prudently spreading our economic, infrastructural, and marketing roots into new, emerging realities.

It is in this way that we can remain ahead of the curve—by nurturing new, exciting, and unique experiences for our visitors. These are trying times, particularly for tourism. But it's precisely why they call for visionary, creative, and realistic tourism policies.

In this context, it is my pleasure and honour to write this foreword. Emily Francis is deeply acquainted with what I call the Malta experience and all its layers. It is from this wellspring of knowledge, from the vantage point of her *Oh My Malta* site, that she so eloquently and lovingly writes about our food products and our farming community. This publication should serve as a textbook case for exploring new vistas for our tourism offer.

—Hon. Clayton Bartolo MP, Minister for Tourism in Malta

Preface

Why should you read this book? I am a film producer and have worked for forty years in the industry. Most of the time I am cut off from reality and immersed in a world where I make others believe what's in front of them. We have an artistic license, so to speak. Most of the time, what's around me I tend to take for granted. I have known Emily, who is from the US, for a couple of years now, and she is living her dream here in the Mediterranean, with us in Malta. I have lived in Malta for most of my life, but rarely do I stop and look at what's around me and enjoy it.

Sometimes you need an anchor to pull you back and help you realise the Joy around you, and Emily is that anchor. She sees what I, and probably most of us who live in the Mediterranean, take for granted and fail to see every day. So coming back to my question...Why should you read this book? Because I say so? No. Because everyone needs a bit of Joy in their life and an anchor to reel them back into reality and enjoy what's around them every day.

—Paul Parker, producer/director,
Paul Parker Productions

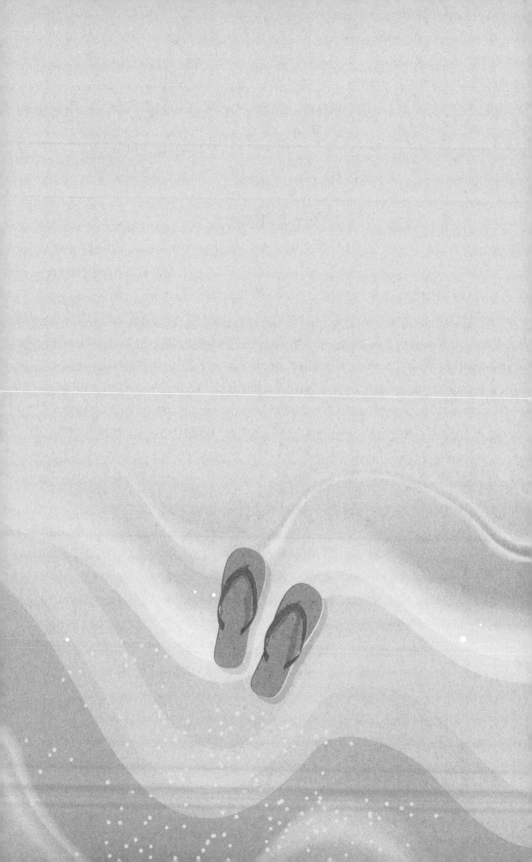

Introduction
The Apéritif

I have a friend who moved to a small town in Colorado many years ago and started working for a bakery. She wrote us a letter telling us all about her new life on the ski slopes. She had just graduated from college and decided that before she entered the corporate world, she would go play somewhere that made her happy. She downsized everything and skied into work every day. She said something in that letter that never left me. She said the words "I found my soul here." I'm not sure my friend would even remember that letter from all those years ago, but I've never forgotten it. I have spent my whole life in search of the place where I would find my soul. That sentence planted a little seed in me from the moment I read it. That seed has been on the hunt for the right place to bloom in my life ever since.

Welcome to the Mediterranean!

My name is Emily Francis. If you have never heard of me before, allow me to introduce myself. I have spent my entire adult life studying anatomy, physiology, and body healing. As a clinically trained bodyworker with extensive specialty training, I have helped hundreds to thousands of people learn to tap into their own sacred body and tune in to the wisdom that the body keeps. *Your body is full of magic and wisdom* has been my tagline. I have given everything I have to the body, the muscles, and how they relate to human emotion. I have followed the spiritual practices that have both saved my life and made my life. Body awareness and body healing will always be a platform that I choose to share. It's what I know best. But there is so much more to a life well lived than what can be gleaned from any single space of focus. I understand that now more than ever after making a life-altering move to Malta and trading in my massage table for a much longer dining table in the Mediterranean.

During the 2020 worldwide madness, my family and I decided to flip the script of our life story and trade in everything we had ever known to make an entirely new life for ourselves. We moved from the south side of the city of Atlanta, Georgia, to the north side of the island of Malta. My husband's company offered us the opportunity to go there and make it our home. In exchange, I do not have a work visa in Malta and cannot be in practice. Mind you, even though I had always kept a handful of clients to work with back home, I had not been in practice full-time for years. Once I had children and got further in my writing career, those became my priorities. Thankfully, my being an author and still hosting my show, *All About Healing*, on Healthy Life Radio remain basically unaffected by this change of location.

Digital roaming allows me to be anywhere in the world and still get to do what I was doing before, even more so now, with the evolution of videoconferencing. All my years of studying healing could not have prepared me for the seismic shift that occurred when I finally found the place in the world that reminded my soul that life is meant to be *relished* instead of simply endured. It was like both an earthquake and a volcanic eruption in my very core. That has been my experience of breaking open and becoming free.

Planting the Seed

My favorite quote about growth is by author Cynthia Occelli: "For a seed to achieve its greatest expression, it must come completely undone. The shell cracks, its insides come out and everything changes. To someone who doesn't understand growth, it would look like complete destruction."[1] The path to get here was one of complete destruction, but the rebuild and restoration have been utterly transcendent. It was such a welcome surprise. There was a whole new life waiting for us in Malta. It was the plot twist in my book of life that I never saw coming.

After many attempts, lots of falls, and lots of searching, giving up, and relenting, that little seed has finally opened up and started to sprout. It's a funny thing with seeds—sometimes you have no idea what will grow out of them. For me now, I'd say that seed looks and feels like a wildflower.

For a long time I struggled to try to accept that maybe I was not meant to have the experience of truly loving the physical environment where I lived. I've known so many people who deeply love where they live and where they are raising their children. I had not been able to fully relate to that feeling until after making this move. The question I asked myself repeatedly over the years was *Why is it that the only people who get to live extraordinary lives are other people? Why not me?* It's not until you find one of the right places for you that you realize how long you had been trying to flourish in a place that was never going to cut it. A common statement from people who have finally found their true love, passion, location, or vocation in life is *I've been in the wrong place long enough to know I'm in the right place now.*

Once you get a taste of something that heightens all your senses, you never want to go back to something that feels dull. This is the case with so many things. Once you taste freedom, you never want to go back to when you felt contained. Once you get a taste of feeling healthy and whole, you want to do everything you can to keep it. Once you taste life in an elevated and radiant capacity, you will do all it takes to eat more from that dish. Once you finally get to taste the experience of being in the right place, there is no turning back to options that simply cannot breathe life into your soul.

Let me ask you this: What would you do if you looked around and realized that where you are is everything you have ever dreamed of

---

1. Cynthia Occelli, on the home page of her website, www.cynthiaoccelli.com.

in most, if not all, areas of your life? What does living the life of your dreams look like to you? Does it have a location? A certain vocation? Does it come with certain faces? I believe that each and every one of us has the option of leveling up in life when we start believing in ourselves and going after our deepest desires. I hope you see that as an option as well.

When timing meets opportunity and you decide to be bold enough to go for it, it can lead to magic. I found my soul in the Mediterranean. The soul experience of elevating the current situation from manageable to sublime will look completely different for each individual. For me, my entire being has woken up in a place where I still catch myself feeling like I stole someone else's dream life. I never want to give it back! Only it's not someone else's dream life. It's not *other people* living an extraordinary life this time. It's me. This one I get to keep.

I love my life in Malta so much. But it is important to note that my life here will never look like your life would if you were here or anywhere else. My paradise might not look like paradise to other people. Even if we were living side by side, we still would not be living the same life. Wherever your joy lives, you have to know that it is meant to be yours and only yours. Where you will find it will be exactly your own path. Trust that there are great delights waiting specifically for you.

Sharing the Secrets of Malta

More than two years ago, I moved to the island of Malta sight unseen with my husband, children, and four animals in the middle of a worldwide lockdown and pandemic. The opportunity presented itself and we took it. I had no way of knowing how it would turn out. I hoped to fall in love with it. I have worked hard at finding my groove here and creating a community of friends. Nothing about this has been easy, but it has all been so worth it.

We live on a tiny island in the Mediterranean that happens to have a heartbeat so big and so loving that it pulled me in and hugged me until its heartbeat could talk to mine. It told me that it is safe here and we will be loved. I feel like the sea herself whispers messages to me every morning when I wake and the moon whispers messages to me at night before I sleep. I make time morning and night to make sure I sit outside with them both. I listen as I thank God for all my lucky stars as I stare out at the magnificence surrounding me. This experience has changed who I am forever. Malta gave me new life. I am beginning to bloom fully alive, in season and on time.

Everyone knows that there are secrets to the Mediterranean lifestyle. The Mediterranean culture lives vibrantly on every coastline and island it touches. There is a lot of wisdom here that can help us simplify, purify, and realize a better way of approaching life. It begins with the diet and culture. It creates healthier and happier people. At least, that is certainly what I had always been taught to believe. Now that I live here, I want to share the secrets I've learned from the people who have lived here for generations.

Since moving here, I have had the most extraordinary opportunities, some of which have presented themselves to me and others that I have handcrafted and created myself. One of my favorite opportunities is that I am now a columnist for the local Malta magazine for tourists, *Oh My Malta*. I write a column titled "Emily in Malta," from the angle of an American woman coming to Malta and interviewing local farmers, fishermen, and chefs about the way that foods are grown, harvested, caught, and prepared on the island. The articles appear monthly in print magazines as well as an online magazine.

When I go to the farms or the fishing village or the smaller sister island of Gozo to meet with the farmers or fishermen, a camera operator and an editor accompany me and I do a live video interview with each guest. I've always been curious about people and what their lives are like, and this work puts me right into the parts of Mediterranean living that I am the most fascinated with: the food practices! It is the most fun I've ever had writing articles! It puts me in a unique position to share authentic information straight from the lifelong farmers and fishermen themselves, people who have dedicated their lives to their family business of delivering that love from their hands to our plates.

Through this new adventure, I have learned so many things that I never could have picked up just from studying or reading about them. I have had my hands down in the soil digging out potatoes and helping pull prickly pears from a cactus. I have picked debris from olives just before they were pressed into oil. I have been on the traditional Maltese fishing boat (a luzzu) and held the most sacred and beloved fish of the island just as my favorite local fisherman arrived back to port. The opportunities that have come to me have been extraordinary, but they are not just for me. They are a gift and a treasure for all of us. It would be selfish of me to keep these long-standing traditions and family gems of wisdom that have been passed down through the generations all to myself.

More than any other time in our recent world history, now is the time to shake things up in all the best ways. The Mediterranean culture and lifestyle teach us that with both food and life, things are best in their most natural state. Living simply, mindfully, seasonally, and naturally as our standard operating system is only the beginning. Adding simple spices can then elevate our lifestyle from the standard to the sublime. If the most recent and turbulent times have taught us anything, it is that there is no more time to waste. If we don't learn how to savor the highs and redirect the lows, we will all be stuck eating only for survival and not for the pleasure it brings.

So many people around the world lost their sense of smell and taste during the pandemic. When a person gets their sense of taste back, what do they want to do right away? They want to eat! They want to eat their favorite foods! They want to eat something that all of their senses can appreciate. They want to eat something that makes them lean back and close their eyes as they hum out loud and savor each delicious bite. *Mmmmm!* Through this book, I want to take that same experience and extend it to our whole lives. I want to introduce you to all the different expressions of flavors in both food and life from the Mediterranean.

What You Will Find Here

This is not a cookbook, but rather a soulful living book where food comparisons are easy to make. It uses food as a directive into the soul, making the book easy to follow and understand. I include some fun recipes and food tips in each chapter, since the Mediterranean is known to be the home of the healthiest diet and lifestyle in the world. And so, with this in mind, I offer you a blend of harvesting and creating a recipe for life that hopefully will wake up your senses and invigorate your soul. We all deserve to live healthy, wild, and free.

Wherever you are in the world, I pray that this offering wakes you up and gives your soul a deep and nourishing hug. If our hearts could hug and hold each other in conversation, my heart would tell yours, "It's not over. It has only just begun. Have faith in what is possible and don't be afraid to add the spice." You might be wondering why I keep referring to food when this is not a cookbook. The answer is simple. What other way can we relate to the idea of feeding our souls? Food ignites the senses as nothing else does. It wakes us up and turns delights into something tangible. In the Mediterranean, food is life. It is a way of life. It is what we eat, what we grow, what we use to nourish, what we use as our love offering. In our home, food is definitely one of our love languages.

Lastly, I use food as our guide because once you get a taste of what life is like when you are truly blissfully and joyfully happy, you will do everything you can to keep it that way. And that is a dish best served fresh, local, and without any added colors, dyes, or preservatives. It is your natural state. You may have forgotten that it's your natural state or maybe what your natural state even feels like. That is what I want to bring back to our table. I also want to remind you that meals are not meant to be eaten alone. Friends and neighbors alike could all use some company and a shared meal.

At the Mediterranean Culinary Academy in Malta, I took a class on spicing up salads and main course dishes from Chef Ariel Guivisdalsky. You will find that he is mentioned and referred to often in this book, because he was my first instructor and he was incredibly generous to meet with me and offer tips and recipes that I weave throughout this book.

Welcome to the Mediterranean way of waking up our souls, feeding them well, and savoring every part of our most precious life! If you are reading this book, it means that you are still breathing. Where there is breath, there is hope. There is still hope for all of us. Now let's go make a really good meal. Mela!

Mela is a word that is used in Malta for practically everything. It can be used for questions, answers, yes, no, thoughts halfway through, angry feelings, happy feelings…it's all one word. There is even a souvenir shop here called Souvenirs That Don't Suck, and almost every shirt in it has only that one word printed on it. The deeply encoded meaning of this single Maltese word is mind-boggling. If you are a true local Maltese, it is likely that the word *mela* will be issued before the rest of any sentence is given. For example, I took driving lessons in order to learn to drive on the opposite side of the road and because driving here is utterly terrifying. My driving teacher, Gordon, always answered my questions like this:

Me: "Gordon, do I turn right or left?"

Gordon: "Mela, left, second exit at the roundabout."

Gordon is so funny that he still sends me random messages just saying in big bold letters *MELA!*

The first time I heard this word as an expression of aggravation was when I was at the post office trying to send a package. The person helping me began with "Mela, mela, mela" as they shook their head at my sheer incompetence in understanding what they were saying to me. Now I use this word to gauge if a person is local. It's the one word that will give someone away every time. I offer it to you and hope that as you read it, it vibrates inside of you and helps to wake you up to something fresh. Let this word serve as your morning coffee as you join me in entering the Mediterranean experience for all things life, love, and happiness. And so it goes.

~Mela!~

Food for Thought

In each chapter, just before I offer a food tip or recipe, we will stop for a moment and take a little snack break. This is an opportunity for you to stop and ponder some of the ideas in each chapter. It's really important to pause and ask yourself questions so you can better identify what your answers to them really are.

Planting the Seed

If you could imagine yourself as a single seed, what kind of seed would it be? Would it be a flower seed? A fruit or vegetable seed? Stop for a moment, close your eyes, and visualize a small seed inside yourself. There is a place inside you that has big dreams and a vibrant imagination. Match your seed to that part of you, and sit with it until you can figure out what it feels like it wants to be. How long will that seed germinate before it cracks open and begins to grow? What colors are inside the seed? What does the seed feel like to you? If we all have something magical and special inside of us, what beautiful, colorful, and joyful seed might yours be? If you can see the seed, will you make a plan to plant it once you recognize its desire for growth?

Food Tip and Recipe

The *apéritif* is my metaphor for the beginning of our journey. This is a way to whet our palate and prepare us for the various courses ahead.

The Apéritif

People in the Mediterranean not only eat in accordance with seasonal foods but also follow a certain recipe for every course of a meal that supports digestion. An *apéritif* is an alcoholic drink that people enjoy before eating to help stimulate their appetite. An *apéritif* is generally a drier type of drink with a lesser amount of sugar, since sugar suppresses the appetite and we are trying to open ourselves up for several courses potentially. The *apéritif* is also usually a low-alcohol drink, because we want to ease our way into the many drinks that might accompany the rest of the courses. Also, the higher the alcohol content of the drink, the duller our taste buds become. We want the *apéritif* to introduce itself to our digestive tract and let it know that we are about to embark on an enticing journey.

A good choice of drink to order before a meal would be a dry martini or dry white wine as opposed to zinfandel, which has a higher alcohol and sugar content. The drink at the end of a meal is called a *digestif*. This is usually more of a brandy, port, bourbon, or sherry. In the final chapter, I include a recipe for limoncello, a typical Mediterranean *digestif*.

The Aperol Spritz (inspired by Aperol)

Created in Venice, Italy, the Aperol Spritz is a typical Mediterranean drink that one can find on most menus as an *apéritif*. Aperol is low in alcohol, at only 11 percent. The liquid is a bright orange color and the taste is vibrant due to its unique blend of herbs and roots. This is an easy cocktail to make at home if you have access to a bottle of Aperol. If not, it can be replaced with a wine or liqueur of your choice. The Aperol Spritz is an orange-flavored drink.

INGREDIENTS
3 ounces (90 ml) Prosecco
2 ounces (60 ml) Aperol
1 ounce (30 ml) club soda
Garnish is usually an orange slice

DIRECTIONS
One variation of the Aperol Spritz uses sparkling water in place of club soda. You can always use a nice dry white wine with the Aperol, along with club soda or sparkling water or seltzer. As long as the Aperol is there, the variations are easy to work with. Now we raise a glass to toast. In Maltese we say *saħħa* (sounds like "sa ha"), which means "to health!" Here's to our health, happiness, and adding in the spice of life from the land of the Mediterranean. Mela!

The Appetizer

"Follow your bliss and don't be afraid,
and doors will open where you didn't
know they were going to be."

—Joseph Campbell, *The Power of Myth*

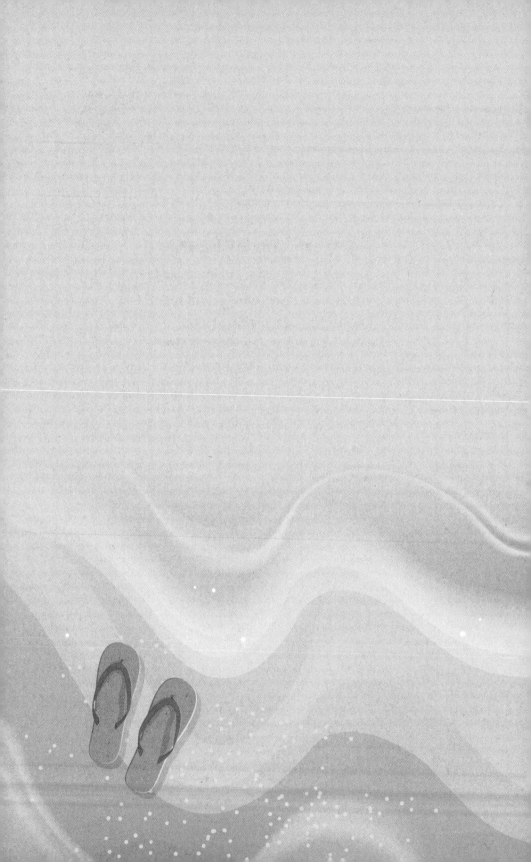

Chapter 1
The Spice of Life

The spices in both food and life are what transform ordinary experiences into something far more gratifying. In this chapter I am going to introduce you to the spices of life that can nourish your mind, body, and soul. We could all do with a little bit of extra spice in our dish.

What Is the Life You Want to Create That Is Going to Feed Your Soul?

The trifecta of spices in Mediterranean dishes is basil, oregano, and thyme—which correlate to the body, mind, and soul, and the elevated experiences of happiness, joy, and bliss. The people of the Mediterranean know more than just how to eat well; they live well. They live in a way that slows down the pace, honors the present moment, puts family first, and embraces friends as part of that family. They know how to add flavor to everything they do. They are loud, are proud of their heritage, know where they came from, and want to invite you in. Anyone who is *good people* is welcome at this long and lovely table. Like the biggest hug of my entire life, I have been embraced by the Maltese people and introduced to the Mediterranean culture in a way that has completely opened up my palate to the greatest flavors of life itself.

Before this experience, I don't know that I would have described myself as a genuinely *happy* person. Most would have described me as cheerful or energetic. Whether or not I was a genuinely happy person, I can say with certainty that I have always been and remain a deeply *grateful* person. Cultivating a gratitude practice is something that can change your life. It saved mine. Being grateful will continue to lead the way in every decision and direction I take in my life, but that won't be the only measurement I will use to assess where I am in my life ever again.

Having a gratitude practice asks that you learn to find peace and contentment in any given situation. I learned how to do that all too well. I subscribed to a teaching that asks you to find a way to be content anywhere. It helps develop a balance inside yourself that allows you to be calm, content, and peaceful wherever you are. It asks that we live our lives through the practice of mindful living. With every step we make, every silence we take, and every shake-up we go through, we quickly bring it back to center, being present as events unfold and always finding the good in any situation. The silver linings abound because we choose to focus on them.

The Art of the Salad

Now that I have lived in the Mediterranean and experienced life from this angle, I can see that cultivating a gratitude practice as the endpoint of mindful living wound up making me satisfied with being simply content. Dare I be so bold as to say that focusing solely on this led me to become complacent. It never asked that I go further and try to explore the levels beyond being simply content. I was never taught to question and evaluate if I was truly happy in my life. I felt more that if I questioned my happiness, I was being ungrateful for all the blessings I already had. But it doesn't have to be one or the other. Questioning our place in our own life is important. It is, in fact, mindful. It is certainly not ungrateful.

Here is a food example of what I mean. Until this year, I feel like I had resigned myself to eating a simple green salad with some jarred blue cheese dressing on top and thinking this was the makings of a decent salad. Most of the time I bought the prepackaged salad with the nuts and berries and the dressing in the packet that you cut and pour. Then I moved to the Mediterranean, where they don't sell pre-made salad dressings or premixed salads for that matter. As an aside for those of us with kids, they also do not sell any boxed macaroni and cheese or pre-packaged pasta dishes. They like things fresh, recently harvested, and delivered from local gardens. You have to learn how to make your own dressing if you want your salad to have it.

I had to learn the art of making a dressing that would make me still want to eat the salad. I hate making my own salads. I always have. I have a lot of strange quirks when it comes to salads. I think everyone else's salads taste better than what I could make, and I rarely order one out in public because I prefer to eat salad with my hands. I hate eating salad with a fork, but I have been getting better at eating it properly when I need to. I love touching every piece of lettuce. I can't explain it. Maybe it's because I use my hands for every opportunity for sensory input that I can get. It's what makes me an extra sensitive and intuitive bodyworker. My hands read the body like it's a storybook written in braille as soon as I make contact. Touch is something extremely precious to me. My hands are my magic tools. Everybody has one—a magic tool within themselves, that is. My hands are mine.

Getting back to making meals, I can make a lot of other dishes quite well, but a simple salad has always eluded me. So being the ever-curious person that I am, and with all this new time on my hands since I am not in practice over here, I took a course at the Mediterranean Culinary Academy on how to spice up a salad. Now, with this learning, consider me transformed into something of a vinaigrette ninja! Seriously, I am now the salad dressing creator in our house. This whole recreating your life thing is very exciting once you get over the initial shock that you will need to figure out who you are and what other things you like to do and then find a way to go do them.

I moved to a place where actual lemons, oranges, and tangerines grow in my own backyard. I learned to make the zestiest and most appealing orange tangerine Dijon mustard vinaigrette dressing to put on top of my spinach salad with dried cranberries and herbed feta. It transforms my plain old green prepackaged salad to something bright, flavorful, and super delicioso. This is a metaphor for life! We can take the prepackaged meal and quickly forget it once we've eaten it, or we can learn how to make something come alive. In the end, either way it's still a salad. It's what we choose to do with it. It's how we choose to make it. That is what makes one dish decent and the other delightful.

The Spices of Happy, Joy, and Bliss

Mediterraneans use a ton of spices without a lot of heat. Most are universal and some are things that I'd never heard of before and made me wonder where they'd been all my life. We will begin simply with the trifecta of any Maltese dish: thyme, oregano, and basil. Those three need to go into a dish together. Using the three together instead of any one of them alone changes the whole flavor profile. It's like long-lost friends finally getting together for a party in your mouth. For people, the trifecta is body, mind, and soul. For what I call the "spices of elevated harmony," it might be happiness, joy, and bliss. There are so many words we could mix into the bowl, but for the three main ingredients of a properly spiced dish, let's stick with these for now.

In my previous books, I offer what I call my Somatic Emotion Chart. *Somatic* means "body," so this is a chart of how our body stores emotions as opposed to how our mind and thoughts access them. In the books, I discuss four heavy emotions and four fabulous emotions that are stored within the body. I differentiate between the levels of happy, joy, connected, and empowered. I did a lot of research on what each of these words mean and how we can apply them to our healing and wholeness. I began to study the ideas behind what happy means, what joy represents, and so on. After my most recent book was released, I did an incredible number of interviews to promote it. I found that in interview after interview I came to the same conclusion: I realized that the biggest and boldest brave new move is to simply allow yourself to sit still when you feel the feelings of happiness or joy and let them be present in your whole body and soul for as long as they are willing to stay.

Why Do We Resist Happiness?

How often do we allow negative self-talk to convince us that we do not deserve to relish the good times in our lives? What is that about? I don't see people here in Malta doing this. It's not what they are taught. They are taught to play when it's time to play and work when it's time to work and not to feel bad about enjoying anything. I now realize that this habit of feeling guilty for being happy is a learned behavior. But why? To control us? To perpetuate self-sabotage? It's enough already! Be happy when you feel happy. For some reason, I think that people have gotten more familiar with sitting inside their grief and trauma than with being able to sit still inside the heart of happiness and joy. Once they can get comfortable inside the joy, that is when a person truly learns the art of savoring the delicacies of life.

Please, let's stop tricking ourselves into believing that if we feel good and vibrant that we will somehow trigger something negative that's been lurking around the corner. Let's not think there's something out there just waiting for us to be happy so it can swoop in and knock us down. It takes real guts to allow ourselves to feel excited and happy! Sometimes it's the most basic concepts in life that we struggle with. This is one of them. Why is "excitement" attached to "scary"? There is so much research to support that what one person experiences as anxiety, another will experience as excitement. The two emotions release the same hormones! What makes one person love it while another runs away in fear? When two people are riding a roller coaster, one will be convinced the wheels are going to come off the rails and kill everyone, while the other will have their arms up and their eyes closed as they scream with delight. They are riding the same ride!

The body experiences both excitement and fear the same way. The adrenaline hormone comes raging out into our bodies while all this is going on. Then we make a choice: Are we enjoying it or are we hating it? Is it excitement or is it terror? Why can't the experience of getting excited and happy be something simple and light like it's intended to be? Please hear me on this: it is a learned response. We are allowed to get excited.

We are allowed to feel free. We have to learn to guard ourselves against being conditioned to believe that we are somehow setting ourselves up for something bad to happen when we choose to feel good.

Happy

According to my research, happiness is something that is externally triggered and joy is something that is deeply felt from the inside. The terms happy and joy are often used interchangeably, but they have their own personalities and energies if you want to get into the nitty-gritty of it.

The research kept bringing me back to the concept of happiness being externally triggered. I think that's because we are taught to build from within (and rightfully so) and not give the outside world as much credit as it might deserve. I truly believe that where we are in the world offers various levels of how happy we can be. This is where we can build up a practice of being grateful, but feeling happy may or may not be easily within reach. Either it becomes something you can almost taste or it is something you can grab and suck down. The experience of happiness is fleeting. It comes in the moment. It is a present-tense emotion. It stays for however long it wants to stay and for however long we open ourselves up to hang on to it. It's not so much stored in the body, but the more we experience it, the more our body and mind begin to recognize it when it comes.

When something is externally triggered, it means it comes from the world outside of yourself, from the world you surround yourself with. This is your basic environment. Does it bring you more or less toward feelings of being happy? Are you living in a location that you love? Start big and work your way in with this one. Are you happy with the country you live in? Are you happy with the state you live in? Are you happy with the part of town you live in? Are you happy with the neighborhood you live in? Are you happy with the home you live in? Are you happy with the people you live with? Are you happy in the place where you work? Keep asking the questions until you find any answers that make you pause and look further.

If you answer no to any of these questions, it might be time to start making plans or coming up with realistic options to change those answers. Then reverse the line of questioning. Where would you be if you were your happiest? Where is your happy place? Is it on an island? On the beach? Near the snow? In your house? With your people? Away from your people? What would your life look like if you were to recreate it brick by brick to bring about feelings of happiness more often?

Joy

Joy is something that your body can store inside the muscle and emotional memory. Joy comes with a deeper sensation. As we feel joy, it attaches itself deeper inside our entire sensory system. We can smell old, familiar smells from a time when joy was triggered and remembered. We can almost go back in time to experience moments in our lives when we felt joy. This emotion is deeply felt and moves through our actual physiology inside. Feeling joy is incredibly vital to our well-being. Doing practices that remind you that you have felt intense joy in your life opens up a channel to both crave and receive more of it.

We don't want joy to live only in our past experiences, however. We also need to ask ourselves how we can create more joy. Who brings you joy? How close are they to you in your life? How easy is it to get to them? What brings you joy? Dance? Art? Music? Photography? Writing? Going to parties? Bowling? What things can you do more of that make your soul feel fully alive? What is stopping you from doing more of them?

Let me ask you this: What is stopping you from trying something that you've always thought about doing but always made excuses for why you couldn't? This is the time to wake yourself up. Stop making excuses and start doing things to create more joy in your soul. It will not show up at your door. You have to go out and find it and create it. Start by asking yourself what that would take, then make your standard list of excuses of why it's not possible. Write them all down. Write every excuse in your book: wrong location, no money, no time, not enough support, etc. Then burn them or tear them up and throw them away.

There is always a way to get some of the things you are dreaming about. Maybe not all of them, but certainly some of them. Let me give you a gentle reminder, however, that as you begin to quest, be sure you are not focusing on the outcome. Finding joy has nothing to do with "I want to be a famous singer." Instead, just sing. Stop projecting what the outcome might be and just go play in whatever it is. That is the house where joy resides.

So many budding writers want to write a book but fear losing their anonymity when they hit the bestseller list and become uber-famous like J. K. Rowling. I love that people think that far out as an option for their work, and I say go for it! But to allow a possibility like that to stop you from ever getting started and writing is ludicrous. Either you love something enough to play deeply in it or you are only attached to what the result might be. The result, even if you become a superstar, will never feed your soul and bring the spice of joy to your life more than the actual process of doing whatever it is will.

Here is an example of what I mean. I love Dr. Bernie Siegel. He is a retired pediatric surgeon and the author of many books, including *Love, Medicine & Miracles*. I have interviewed him on my radio show several times. One of the things he always talks about is how he encourages people who are living with cancer to go and do something they truly love to do, something that brings their soul alive. If they have always wanted to play violin, for example, or they used to in their younger years but forgot about it, he tells them to get back to it.

Dr. Bernie has observed that many times the practice of finding soul-feeding joy has saved their lives. Patients defy the odds again and again when they have something more meaningful to live for. This in no way negates wanting to live longer because you have people in your life you want to live for. I am talking about something that is only for yourself and your sacred spirit. That is the focus of the spice of joy here.

Have you ever heard the story of a man who closed his law practice as soon as he was diagnosed with cancer and started playing the violin again and added years to his life, joining the local orchestra and completely defying his initial prognosis? And another story of a man who moved to Colorado because he had always dreamed of living there and defied his initial prognosis? (Hint: you have heard these stories if you've read Dr. Bernie's books or listened to him on my show.) When Dr. Bernie called the man's family to find out why he had not been invited to the funeral in Colorado, the man himself picked up the phone! He told Dr. Bernie, "It was so beautiful here I forgot to die." I asked Dr. Bernie about this story again when he was last on my show and he said something that I wrote down in hopes of sharing it. He said, "Let your heart make up your mind." Joy is a spice of life that is best served with purpose. Living in line with purposeful joy can save you. Go find what it is that reminds you that you are alive, creative, and oh-so-mighty. Then go do so much more of that.

We are not getting any younger, and whatever it is you want to do that wakes you up to being more fully alive, go get to it! What are you waiting for? Make a deal with yourself right now while you are reading this that today you will at least start to do some research on how to get yourself into something new and exciting. If you want to make more friends who have similar passions, this is exactly how you do it. Once you get started and show up, you will enter a new community of other brave souls who are also looking for something more joyful in their lives. That is exactly how you find them. You show up first.

Bliss

Now let's go to another word that describes the goodness and highs of emotions and experiences within ourselves: *bliss*. What does bliss mean in relation to happy or joy? According to the *Oxford Dictionary*, bliss is "perfect happiness; great joy."[2] This trilogy looks a lot to me like basil, oregano, and thyme. It's not the same thing, but together these three emotions elevate each flavor into something new and more delicious. Again, these three words are commonly used interchangeably, yet they still each have their own personality and energy.

2. Oxford University Press, s.v. "bliss," accessed August 2022, available at https://www.lexico.com/en/definition/bliss.

Bliss as I know it comes from my years of study of yoga. In traditional yoga philosophy, there is a term we use when someone dies. We say that the person has entered *mahasamadhi*, which translates to "perpetual bliss." It is the place you enter once you leave your body. When the word *bliss* comes to me, I can't help but think of this terminology. Another Sanskrit word that is one of my favorites is *satchitananda*, which translates to "existence, knowledge, and bliss." Because of my years of study of yoga philosophy and the recurring use of the word *bliss*, I tend to associate the concept of bliss with a whole-body experience beyond happy or joy.

What if we decided that bliss translates to heaven on earth instead of another place beyond this life? What if bliss lives right here in this very moment while we are alive and shifting? What if bliss is what happens when we choose to savor the good things and swallow them whole and allow them to nourish us and wake up all our senses? What if bliss lives inside the food we eat, the thoughts we think, and the movements we make? What would it be like to taste bliss? What would a little bite of bliss taste like to you? What would that flavor profile be?

To be able to find your sweet spot in life to taste your bliss, happiness, and joy is something that only the bravest of us might be called forth to explore. Or maybe we didn't even realize it was possible because we've been operating on autopilot for so long that we didn't even know that we had it in us. When I say that, I realize how absurd that thought is considering the massive, earth-shattering changes that all of us have had to make over the last few years with the global pandemic.

Change has come and will continue to come. Just like the waves of any sea, they endlessly ride up and back. Some days are brutal, while other days are still. We learn to surf them or bust. In these waves of uncertainty, illness, climate change, violent behavior, and angry people, what can bring you to the table that is serving your personal recipe for those sweet little bliss bites? What changes do you want to make that could elevate you higher than automatic pilot? Then there are the bigger questions: What changes are you willing to make to get there? What are you doing that is not feeding your soul? Don't you owe it to yourself to find out what life would taste like if you did get there?

What if we throw happy, joy, and bliss into a mixing bowl and create a new dish with them? What would it taste like to our souls? The happiness from the world around you (body), the joy from the world within you (mind), and the bliss to elevate it to heaven on earth (soul) in food form? Because that is the dish I want us all to start serving. Pull out the good china—it's time to sit down and savor the next plate.

Food for Thought: Some Questions to Ponder

Feel free to write the answers to these questions right here on this page.

If you were to live your happiest, healthiest, very best life…

- Where would you be?
- What would you be doing?
- Who would you be?
- How would you be?
- How would you play?

Food Tip and Recipe

Once you know how to make a simple vinaigrette dressing, it becomes much easier to play around with the ingredients to fit the flavor profile of any given salad. The simplest rule is that in a vinaigrette, it's ¼ vinegar to ¾ oil and the rest adds flavor and texture to balance out the acidity. Here are three very simple salads, one from Italy and two from Greece. The Greeks have very serious rules about what goes together in their salad bowls.

Citrus Dijon Vinaigrette Dressing
(Recipe by Ariel Guivisdalsky)

INGREDIENTS

1 organic orange, lemon, or tangerine (or mix and match)

Zest of all the peel of one piece of fruit, plus the juice of one or more (if you are using more than one variety of fruit)

¼ cup (60 ml) apple cider vinegar (or whatever vinegar you wish)

2–3 tablespoons Dijon mustard (depending on your preference)
¾ cup (175 ml) olive oil (preferably extra virgin)
Pinch of sea salt
Pinch of pepper

Optional Additions:
Tahini (I love to add about a teaspoon of tahini or more as needed to
    thicken the dressing.)
1 clove fresh garlic, minced or chopped
Any fresh herbs you want to add

Sicilian Simple Salad: Blood Orange Salad with Fennel (Recipe by Salvatore Romano)
INGREDIENTS
Blood orange slices
Fennel, fresh and chopped
Spring onion, thinly sliced
Drizzle with the olive oil of your choice (but the Dolce di Rossano is
    always an easy option for guests and friends).

Greek Village Salad (Recipe by Loukia Makou)
INGREDIENTS
Tomato
Spring onion
Cucumber
Kalamata olives
Green peppers
Feta cheese
Oregano
Salt
Olive oil
*No lemon

DIRECTIONS

Loukia says, "When you make a Greek salad with feta, tomatoes, and cucumber, you don't use lemon. But if you make a salad with lettuce, spring onion, dill, and cucumber, you can add olive oil with lemon or olive oil with vinegar, whatever you prefer." A very serious Greek rule that I've been taught now more than once or twice is that you never put lemon and feta in the same bowl! Lemon does not go with tomato either. I had no idea! It's a flavor match deal, I'm assuming.

The final rule for all Greek salads is this: Once you've finished any salad with olive oil, you drop your bread into the bowl and allow it to soak up all the extra oil that's left over. People here are not on a diet; there are no restrictions. Olive oil is welcome and invited and not measured. This is a perfect strategy for living well: take that bread and drop it to the bottom and soak up all the goodness that's been waiting for you to enjoy.

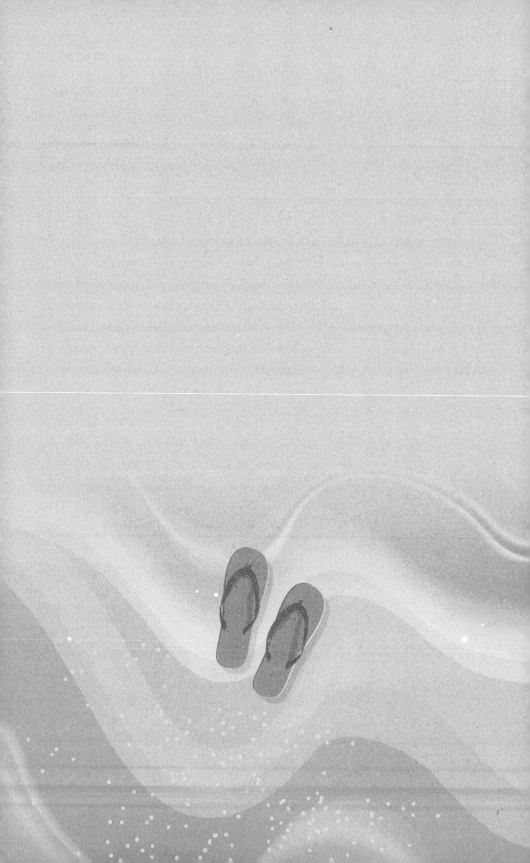

Chapter 2

Get Comfortable Outside Your Comfort Zone

Comfort zones keep us small. Aren't we tired of playing down the role we serve in our own lives? There is never a need to be a supporting character in our own story. We are the lead, the director, and the narrator. Never hand off any one of those to anyone else.

We have to learn to take ourselves less seriously and become brave enough to allow our edges to hang out more often. The parts of us that feel more vulnerable to criticism no longer need to be tucked in. Get uncomfortable, get dirty, get messy, and let yourself have a little more fun. You teach others how to see you simply by changing your view of yourself. This will, in effect, change the world around you.

Not everything has to be so strictly defined, and this includes you. Feeling contained makes us feel like we can't breathe, and I want us to get out of our self-created containers and take a deeply needed breath of fresh air. Reconnect with the outside world and the wonders of nature to wake up your soul and remind yourself that the world is a mighty big place and there is more than one way that you can fill your space in it. You are a valuable and sacred part of this world, and nothing would look the same without you in it.

Get Your Hands Dirty and Your Feet Bare

The term *earthing* is from the study of environmental medicine, which examines how factors in the outside world can negatively influence a person's health. In the study of earthing, or *grounding*, it has been shown through actual scientific research that having direct physical contact with Mother Earth and her electrons can positively influence a person's health in tremendous ways. It's known as "electric nutrition" when you try to get barefoot for a minimum of five minutes a day to influence your health and wellbeing. The earth's surface is covered with electrons, and those electrons can influence our health in ways ranging from regulating our sleep to reducing physical pain, decreasing cortisol levels, regulating our internal body clock, reducing chronic illness, and promoting an over-all sense of peace and wellness within the various circuits of the body.[3] When we play in the dirt with our hands or walk barefoot upon the earth, the electrons make their way into our bodies to help us become healthier and happier versions of ourselves.

I am firmly convinced that this is why all the farmers I meet are happier, calmer, more balanced, and lovely to be around. They play in the dirt every single day! They are earthing all day long! I live in a house with several fruit trees on the property. I remember being told that the soil here is extremely rich in nutrients, but it wasn't until I heard it repeatedly from various farmers that I understood this more clearly.

The soil here is so rich in nutrients and so alkaline due to the deposits from the limestone that putting our hands down in it or feeling that soil beneath our bare feet can have such an incredible impact on our whole sense of wellbeing. After a good rain, the soil feels like a sponge. You step onto it and your foot drops down at least a few inches. It's incredible and like nothing I've ever experienced before. You can practice earthing by digging in the dirt, walking through the grass anywhere, potting plants, or walking along the sand. The electrons will ride up into your whole body. When you are barefoot by the water and put your hands in the

3. Chevalier, "Earthing."

sand, it's like you can magically feel your whole body balancing in the joy! Maybe it's more than just the simple pleasure of being at the beach or by the water; maybe it's the whole electric nutrition process that is happening in those moments without us even realizing it.

Whether you are walking barefoot on the earth or playing with your bare hands in the dirt or sand, the electrons are absorbed by the body the same way. Now imagine that these farmers are getting a stream of electrons from their hands and feet as they are outside so much of the time filling their bodies with earthly magnificence. They are the true *salt of the earth* people, and I celebrate them in ways I never imagined before witnessing it in real life.

Even if you don't live anywhere near a place with water, we all have the sky above. Everyone has access to the natural world: grass, dirt, rocks, etc. Everyone can plant in small planters and play in the soil. Everyone can walk outside and be barefoot and take in the natural world and the healthy electrons. Everyone can open a window. Almost everyone has access to trees, where the air is richer and oxygen is being handed to you by every leaf. Even in a place like New York City you have Central Park, where you can go to feel the magic of nature and rebalance yourself. Nature is everywhere in some form. Do what you can daily to connect with it.

The Farmer and the Land

The farmers here are outside from the wee morning hours with their hands directly in the dirt and breathing in fresh air from the soil, the sky, and the sea winds. It doesn't get any healthier than that! This is exactly what produces some of the happiest and healthiest people in the world. Their stress levels are very different from that of, say, a corporate person who is constantly pressured by deadlines and performance reviews, stuck in an office with possibly no windows and no access to fresh air.

This is not to say that the farmers do not have stress, because of course they do! They get stressed by the weather and the massive changes that are happening to our climate. They get stressed by how much they can produce for each crop daily and getting them into people's hands. They stress over the many months that don't have rain and they gather every drop during the months that do. They are always planning and preparing for best- and worst-case scenarios.

This year we had more rain in Malta than in the last sixty years. The farmers who planted their strawberries early lost their entire crop for the upcoming season. It was all wiped out with one big storm. When it rains here, it is torrential. One big rainstorm can take it all out depending on where it lands. Last year I tried to buy olive oil from a large family business set up on a side road. When I went in, they told me that because of a storm the previous year, all their olive trees had been damaged and did not produce enough oil to sell. Thankfully this year they had oil to sell again. These farmers are at the complete and total mercy of the weather. As the climate continues to change, it is wreaking havoc on the lands.

Joseph, a tomato farmer in Malta whom I interviewed, says that he wakes up every morning at 2:00 a.m. to pick the ripe tomatoes and get them delivered to the markets in the middle of the night so the produce can be the freshest that we can buy on the island. Once he drops off the produce at the fresh market, it is separated and distributed to the shops and markets and placed on the shelves before our morning alarms have even gone off. It is incredibly tedious work and doesn't offer much time for rest. They work as long as the crops are growing. They don't miss their opportunities with ripe produce. They don't let any of it get rotten on the trees.

This kind of life, though simpler and healthier in many ways, can be exhausting and requires a serious commitment to the earth and its people. I have so much more awareness and respect when I am eating these beautifully tended foods grown locally. I feel the love inside every bite. This offers a depth to mindful eating that I'd never had before meeting my new beloved friends here and learning how the different foods grow. This is their love language, and they speak it quite fluently.

The Ingredients Basket

Have you ever watched food shows where the contestants get a basket with the same combination of odd ingredients and their job is to turn them into something delicious? Somehow they all manage to make something really good but also very different with the same set of starting ingredients. They choose different spices to add and different ways to prepare each item, and many times they come up with something really surprising with each basket.

These contestants can pull off some really solid dishes with the spices and flavors they are trained to use. Chefs and home cooks alike from all over the world go on these shows to create their native dishes from the basket of ingredients that will knock the judge's socks off. They know what to do and when to do it when it comes to adding the spices at just the right time to elevate each ingredient. It is surprising how many different plates are presented with such different flavors and cooking methods starting with the same simple ingredients. That combination of ingredients is the one constant, and what the contestants choose to bring into that dish with them makes all the difference.

You are always the constant denominator of your story. You are the basic ingredient in what can become the most elevated, succulent, and delicious dish you have ever tasted. But those dishes don't just happen. It takes knowledge, awareness, perseverance, and constant presence to transform a simple ingredient into something powerful, spicy, and tasty. That same simple ingredient sitting on your plate could just as easily become burned, bland, soggy, or overdone if you don't know what to do with it or you lose focus of what you are trying to create. It all starts as the same single ingredient: you. What you choose to do with your life going forward is entirely up to you. You always have the choice to elevate the flavors. If you feel lost, soggy, or burned out, you can change direction.

You can always choose to learn more about what you are working with and what you are trying to create both on your plate and in your life. For example, if you take one boneless, skinless chicken breast, some potatoes, and a few vegetables, you will have a full meal. How you cook the chicken will affect the texture of it but not necessarily the taste. You can bake it, broil it, steam it, or whatever you like and it will have the same basic taste when you bite into it—until you change the spices that you add to it. Add some oregano, thyme, marjoram, basil, and rosemary and all of a sudden it's an Italian chicken. Add some saffron and smoked paprika with a little salt and pepper and now it's a Spanish chicken. You can prepare a chicken breast in a thousand different ways, with just as many styles. There are not that many different ingredients in the world, but there are many spice combinations and cooking styles that can make any starting point come alive in a bold new way. Change can be really scary, but it also can be uplifting and liberating. And changes that you choose to make don't always have to be permanent. Sometimes you just need a little change of scenery to put things in perspective.

Nothing is stopping us from learning how to create something better with our lives that lends more flavor to what we are currently cooking up. You are the combination of every flavor and layer that you add to your life. You are the reflection of where you have been, who you have been influenced by, where you are going, and what you want to become. These things don't just happen. You have to make them happen. Whatever flavor profile you want to become, it is within reach if you want it to be and you choose to make it so.

The Caterpillar Makes the Wings

We morph in and out of what we need and want to be during different phases of life. We cocoon when we need to go inward and we fly when it's finally time to find freedom in the outside world. In between those times, we do a lot of introspection, creating, growing, and building within ourselves to be released into a new place, one where we are not held in such tight captivity. Those different phases of life are vital to our soul's growth and restoration. When you are in a cocoon state, don't allow that time to go to waste. It is a precious part of any level of growth and transition. It may feel cramped and miserable while you are inside of it, but that is part of the journey. You can't jump to the flying part without going through the phases required to get you airborne.

Everything you are feeling and learning and growing into matters. It matters for your soul's evolution and for all the potential ripple effects of your actions in the world. We all have the opportunity to change the plate in front of us and add different and more unique spices as we go. When you come out of hiding and decide to go after what you want, it can be tricky, and you must come out wiser and more open to what is happening around you. You will need thicker skin and resilience that you may not have been comfortable with before. But it's your life and it is entirely your choice what to do with it going forward. We can use the downtime to build our wings for strength, stamina, and endurance. And when the timing lines up, we need to trust that we have everything it takes to fly.

When the Wings Expand

When you do finally leave the cocoon and put yourself back out there and start exploring the avenues that create a more open pathway, you will likely run into some hurdles. Just because we may come out stronger or even wiser doesn't mean it will somehow be easier. It might even be more challenging. This is likely because at some point in the time you took to prepare yourself to fly, you leveled up in your growth. The challenges presented ahead will reflect the new advances you've made.

But with an increase in challenges, there might come greater rewards. No change will come at zero cost. It will cost you your comfort. It will cost you an array of things, but you must choose what is most important to you. The more you allow yourself to take risks, the more likely it is that you will reach new opportunities. Trust that there is a place that can feed your soul and offer you an elevated existence and everything that comes with it. The trick is to allow for this flow to happen and then have the insight and courage to step into it once you see it moving.

Above all, you must trust that you have grown strong wings and can handle the new adventures as they come. This is when you become an active participant in your personal experience. Then suddenly you find that you have entered a state that flows more readily. Conditions change and things free up a bit in a way where you can notice them and handle them. This does not require a move or even a change in location. It asks that you open up to the possibilities that you are specifically designed to be able to create and accomplish. People all around the world have created exceptional new avenues of creativity and income by using social media platforms. This is more about letting yourself explore within yourself what you really want to be doing with your time and how you want to divide it up.

There is the option of a career path that heightens. There is a soulful path that is elevated. There is a love path that radiates. When we push too hard, the offerings become less visible. When we don't push hard enough, they are barely a glimmer. Maybe we stop pushing altogether and learn to allow ourselves to elevate from a different flow of life. We tend to put so much pressure on ourselves to perform any given task, and instead maybe we should allow the pressure to go down to the bottom and allow our soulful nature and curiosities to rise up. It requires a certain finesse to be able to understand the difference between making a path and allowing the path to be created. When you learn to balance better by working hard, playing often, resting well, and trusting the whole process, new opportunities will be created and presented when you least expect it. Things will show up when you do. And when an opportunity shows itself to you, I want you to go surfing.

Put Yourself Out There

When I moved to Malta, I reached out to local magazines and newspaper outlets to see if I could write for them. I knew I had a really interesting perspective and wanted to share anything that would support building a platform in my new beloved home. I tried a couple of places to no avail. Then I emailed the local magazine I write for now and got exactly the right person to respond. This was a case of opportunity meets divine timing. I am thoroughly convinced that had anyone else been the one to receive my email, none of this would have happened. It had to be Amy.

Not only did Amy open up to giving me a shot to write, but she wanted to put me on camera! She wanted me to write each article and go with her and their camera operator and interview local farmers on camera. Oh, how badly I wanted to do this! Somewhere long ago, this used to be my dream! I used to dream about doing things on camera and would imagine myself doing it. But I also realize I did very little to put myself out there and make that happen. I was never intentionally clear about what I wanted and therefore not within reach of a path that would create it. I never had enough confidence in the way I looked to be able to go after this dream in a way that would garner real results.

In the previous few years of book publishing and trying desperately to have a voice that carried my message, I made a promise to myself to say yes to every single opportunity that presented itself to me. This was no exception. I said yes right away when this person asked me to find and set up an interview with a local potato farmer after I told her how delicious I found the local potatoes to be. In between the moments of saying yes and showing up, how quickly every thought of how fat and old and horrible I would look came rushing into my head!

My inner critic can be outright vicious. The other voice in my head, however, has done an extraordinary amount of healing, personal work, and self-reflection, which gave me the confidence I needed to trust that I was exactly the right person for this new opportunity and I had everything I needed to make it come to life and do us all proud. I had to believe that this opportunity came to me for a reason, and I owed it to myself to find out just what that was. As the great George Eliot is often quoted as saying, "It's never too late to become what you might have been." So I went for it. I turned away from the inner dialogue that loves to shoot me down and went for it anyway.

Digging for Jewels: The Maltese Potato

One of my dearest friends on the island opened a small café with her husband just months before the first wave of Covid hit. The timing could not have been worse, and no one could have predicted it. We started eating there every Sunday in support once they were able to open back up. She served a dish to me and mentioned that these were local Maltese potatoes. I hadn't paid much attention to whether I was eating local potatoes before that moment, but once I tried them, it was a done deal. Now we only buy potatoes with the St. John's Maltese cross somewhere on the bag. If they are not produced locally, we try not to buy them. The local ones taste both richer and cleaner somehow. Digging them out of the dirt is like hunting for treasure. When you dig them out, because of the quality of the soil, the potatoes are so clean that it doesn't look real. They look like they were already washed and then put back in the soil just for show.

I am very interested in potatoes for many reasons. One, if you left me on a deserted island and I could choose only three foods to bring with me, I would choose potatoes, eggs, and chocolate. Two, I watched a TV show several years ago that talked about how a standard American potato goes through several rounds of bleaching and spraying with pesticides before it ever reaches your plate.[4] Since I am now living in a GMO-free country (GMO = genetically modified organism), potatoes were my first food of interest. I found a farmer who grows the potatoes for Air Malta. Just finding this man was a big story in and of itself. I had to track down the marketing department for the airline in the Netherlands to help me locate my farmer in Malta.

My first interview with Paul, the potato farmer, was beyond amazing. What a gentle heart and massive charm this man has! I adore him and think of him still almost daily. He was my introduction to Maltese farmers and exactly why I have grown to love them all so much. After I called Paul to set up our interview time, he said to me, "Now remember, I am Maltese, which means if you get lost anyplace on the island, just call me and I will come to pick you up and bring you here!"

When I showed up for the first interview that day and met the team in person, all I could see was that Amy, the editor, was twenty years my junior, as well as tan, long, lean, and gorgeous. I assumed it would be

---

4. Dr. Oz Show, "Organic Grocery List: Potatoes."

a one-time gig for me, because I know I look better on my media sites than in person. I know exactly what angles to photograph myself at, and although I don't use filters like I probably should, I also don't post photos that are not flattering. Then as we started, she turned to me and said, "OMG, this is awesome. You've got to do all foods from now on!"

And that was it. I was now being asked to be in a place that I would have killed for many years ago, when I was cuter, younger, and in much better physical shape. Now I'm a middle-aged mother who gave up the dream a long time ago of ever being on camera for anything I was pursuing. And yet timing is everything and this is really happening!

Bold, Brave, and a Bit of a Stalker

Every interview I have done in Malta has been something of a wild goose chase in searching for the right person and then letting go and trusting the process of finding not just someone, but exactly the person who is meant to be there with me. Just because I have a column in a magazine does not mean they hand me a contact list of everyone I need to interview. It is entirely up to me to think of a food and then go find a farmer who grows it. I have had to be relentless in chasing down each interview. I have been told by people to go to a farming town and sit at the local coffee shop across from *the church on the square* (there is a large church on literally every town square, so this is a very real location as the starting point) and then find myself a farmer to speak to.

As it happens, across from the big church on the square of one particular farming town is an actual coffee shop that is aptly named the Farmer's Coffee Shop. And later I found that in that same town there is a place called the Farmers Bar. Maybe one is for the morning and one is for the afternoon. That seems simple enough. Take myself down there and start asking questions from table to table? Sometimes I feel more like a stalker when I set out to track these people down!

Never have I had to be so bold and brazen to invite myself into people's lives, especially because it appears that the majority of farmers and fishermen speak Maltese more than they speak English. Those are the two official languages of this country. There are plenty of people who are instantly turned off when I come along speaking my American English and try to convince them to invite me, an editor, and a camera operator to their home or farm so I can ask them questions about themselves. Unfortunately for me, English is the only language I speak fluently. This is when I hand off to my editor for translation. She and I make an incredible team. She has the brains and boldness to create such a thing, and I am the ballsy American who will go to great lengths to make it happen. Together we make it work.

This job has been an incredible lesson in putting myself out there and going outside my comfort zone. I'm getting better and better at walking up to random strangers, introducing myself, and asking for help. To my great surprise, so far each person I've found to interview has been just the right choice. It has never been easy to find someone, but the outcome has been fruitful every time. The way things keep turning out for us makes us trust the process more as we go. I knock on an insane number of doors to create these opportunities, and for that, I am developing a thicker skin and relentless persistence.

I'm also refusing to take no for an answer. If I get a no from one person, I don't walk away or hang up the phone without asking if they know someone else they would recommend. Now that I have met enough farmers, I can finally call one to help me get to the next, and the next. They tell them that *I'm good people*, and from there, more have opened themselves up to receive my invitations. It's been the most fun I've ever had getting to meet so many incredible people this way.

During these last two years that I have been writing this column, my work with the magazine has evolved. The editor I first worked with, Amy, stepped away from her position. Now, working with Philippa, we have opened up the column to expand beyond single ingredients and interview food and drink makers. Some of these newer articles have included specialty foods for the village feasts and festas, restaurants and local pasta makers, local brewers, and even the prison bakery. The column has grown up with us.

I'm finding a way to trust the path forward, but I also don't sit back and expect it to happen for us. No one is going to hand me these interviews on a platter. Not being local to the country makes some things nearly impossible, while at the same time and to the same degree, being a foreign tour guide adds just enough spice to me that people are curious enough to show up.

Ask New Questions

All of a sudden I was asking myself totally new questions, like *What would you want to do if you could find a way to make it happen?* This is not to be confused with that old question *What would you do if you knew you could not fail?* Failure is always part of the process. No one just walks in without any effort or without experiencing some setbacks that brought them to that place. It's a given and one that we all need to swallow and digest because it's not going away. Falling down is always part of the climb. What I'm asking myself now is *What would I want to do if I was able to find a way to bring it to life?*

These questions are not strictly for me, of course, but are questions for you to answer for yourself. Do you have the strength, the courage, the fortitude, the follow-through, and the will to leap into something bigger than what you are currently doing? And what exactly would that something bigger be? What does the story look like when the voices in our heads are no longer telling us that someone—everyone—would do it better? Start asking yourself new questions. It's the first step in formulating a plan that will bring about the changes you seek. We all deserve to be happier and to live more wildly without so many restrictions. Be brave and bold and willing to take it up a notch! Throw in that new spice and see what it does!

The truth is, I asked to write a column. I thought that was being brave and bold. Going to the level of being on camera is something I never saw coming. But I dance joyfully in the fun and the insights that I am privy to because of this opportunity. It has opened up a whole new world for me over here. To sit down with such incredible people who carry so much wisdom and history is an enormous privilege. People here love that we are showcasing their own. The locals are very protective of their country, their land, and most especially their people. My coming in and highlighting this rather than criticizing it has been outrageously rewarding for me personally and professionally and, most especially, for everyone we've highlighted. Together, we are building something so special that I have to pinch myself to make sure it's real.

Let It Grow

There is another part of this idea of putting ourselves out there that is important to note. Asking ourselves the right questions about what we want in our lives is important. Taking steps to make those ideas a reality is also important. Allowing the forms to shape and shift without trying to direct where they go is paramount. It's not just putting ourselves out there; it's allowing whatever energy we put out to move around and grow beyond what we can see in the short view. We are all control freaks to some degree, and we love to try to control the outcome of nearly everything we do.

If you loosen your grip and allow the energy you put forth to grow as it's meant to and beyond your immediate expectations, you may be surprised. There are baby steps we can take when we move into a new dimension of our lives. We first want to commit ourselves to taking that first step in the direction we have thought about and decided on. Then we need to formulate a plan to make it happen and step into that pathway. Once we begin, we have to change the way our mind wraps around our every move. Cut everything into bite-size pieces, and do one piece at a time. When each step or piece has been put into motion, become very clear with yourself to allow that seed to grow without you standing over it waiting for it to bloom. The old adage "A watched pot never boils" applies here for every step we make. I have to remind myself of this adage time and again when I find myself getting antsy while trying to manage my expectations of any given effort. Trusting the process requires great faith in the process itself. Find a place within yourself where you feel both comfortable and confident. Do not attach yourself to specific outcomes, for that can limit what things can become. There are plenty of ways for our efforts to grow that exceed our limited vision. Do not block the process and smother the opportunities that glide alongside your efforts.

For example, at the time that I was writing this chapter, I was asked to be on a local food show in Germany because they saw my article on a type of cheese made in Malta and Gozo. The Maltese or Gozitan cheese known as *ġbejna* is a delicacy that is handcrafted by locals and tastes truly sublime. It is one of the signature foods of the Maltese. Of course I said yes to the offer! Never could I have imagined that opportunity presenting itself, as it was nowhere even near my peripheral vision. It grew out of itself. It arrived because a TV producer was looking for food interviews to do in Malta and my name came up on her search and she reached out.

The efforts you make can build on themselves if you stop blocking the process. For every step you take out of your comfort zone and into the wild unknown, something grows and expands in a direction you might not be able to see right away, but you have to trust it. Trust that anything can grow out of itself if the seeds have been planted. Trust in the strength of the seeds that you plant and let the rest take care of itself. It will grow if you step back and allow that seed to sprout.

For me, it was just a quick TV spot, but who knows what else might come out of it? Someone else could see it and decide to reach out. A year earlier, no one from a TV show from another country would have had any way of finding me. Now, because I am writing these food articles, I am putting something out into the world that has a chance to grow into any number of things. Anything can happen if you plant the seeds and stand back to let them grow.

Are You Good People?

People here in Malta are more concerned with your level of character and what interesting things you bring to the table than anything else. They are not nearly as concerned with what you do as with who you are. *Are you good people?* If the answer is yes, then that's all they need to know.

I have had more opportunities, all on camera, in the last year than I had over the previous ten back home. And I have figured some of it out. Maybe I am now in a place where being a short, round, loud, fun, charismatic, wildly curious American writer who is madly in love with all things Malta is a welcome breath of fresh air!

I don't know about you, but I got tired of playing small in my own life. I got tired of letting the voices of fear and negativity control the narrative. I got tired of trying to fit into places that never supported and elevated who I was always meant to be. I know I'm not alone in these thoughts. I've had to battle my negative thought patterns and fearful thoughts to step up and do this. I cannot let opportunities like this pass me by just because I'm dwelling on all my flaws while the people around me are highlighting my strengths. The voices in my head can be ruthless. However, the countervoice in my head has done a ton of personal work and has decided that the mean monster that still likes to rear its ugly head does not get to be the voice that wins.

I know it is common for those of us who put ourselves out there in the public eye to be subjected to more or maybe louder criticism. It's the nature of the beast. I also know that many times those who choose never to put themselves out anywhere may be subjected to even more criticism from inside their own minds than anyone on the outside could ever dish out. This is something we need to support each other on. We need to be happy with who we are and have confidence in what we bring to the table. And if you can't find anything interesting or fun to bring to the table, it's time to get out there and create an updated version of yourself. Everyone is awesome most of the time. Everyone is exciting some of the time. Everyone has something special and beautiful and unique about them all of the time. Focus on those parts of yourself. Be willing to take a bite into something new and discover how it tastes.

Almonds

There are almond trees that line the roads in many places around the island of Malta, including one that hangs over my own backyard. Though

I doubt there is any single reason for it, I always seem to find the almond trees very close to the prickly pear cactus. Maybe it's because they are both sun lovers and heat seekers. When the almonds appear, they are wrapped in a peel that is a soft greenish color that looks fuzzy on the outside. Just under the peel is a hard shell called the husk.

Interestingly enough, I was speaking with a grower who mentioned that here in Malta, we have two kinds of almonds: one that is very sweet and one that is absolutely disgusting and not edible. How to tell the difference? You have to take a bite and find out! There are no distinguishing characteristics between the two outside of tasting them. Their leaves look the same, the trees are the same, and the colors of the skin and husk all look the same. There is not even a difference in smell. There is no other way to know that one is nasty and the other is tasty except to stick your tongue out, give it a swipe, and then take a bite.

Art imitates life, and so does food. You might think something looks just like the sweet thing you are seeking only to find out once you taste it that it makes your mouth hurt as you cringe in disgust. When we choose a path, we won't know where it leads until we are firmly on it. You can't know which path leads to the sweet and which tastes nasty until you are far enough into it that it can be revealed to you. You just have to take the chance and trust that among the nasty ones you will be able to find something sweet, too. There are many ways to get to the destination you are seeking within your soul. No one set path has to be it. Trust that if you find yourself going down a path that shows itself to be inadequate, there will be other options for you to try. You just have to be willing to take that first bite and find out.

The Lost Art of the Prickly Pear

The prickly pear is a prime example of something that has an insane amount of surprise and delight hidden beneath a somewhat defensive exterior. Cacti grow all over the Mediterranean, with the dry weather and extreme heat. On most of our cactus plants grow beautiful wildflowers that make way for the prickly pear to bloom in late spring into the summer.

We have a cactus growing in our backyard. I was warned early on not to touch them because they have prickles that are very painful. As the prickly pears began to rot and fall to the ground, I thought to myself, "If I just pick them up by each dry end, that shouldn't hurt, right?" Wrong. From far away it does look as though their large prickles could be painful but also possibly avoidable depending on where you grab them. This is totally false. The prickly pear is covered in tiny little hairlike needles on every single part of its skin. Once you get close enough to touch them, I swear it's like the hairs jump off and pin themselves up and down your arms and hands. It took me days to get every little hair out of my skin.

From then on, I stayed away from this fascinating plant in our yard. That is, until I scoured the island to find the perfect farmer, Tony, to interview about the allure of the prickly pear. The art of the prickly pear in finding the beauty within all comes down to how you slice it. The pear, without ever being cut open and exposed, holds inside it this gorgeous, vibrant, surprising color and flavor just waiting for a person wise enough to know how to get in there and find them. Isn't that the case with us so often in our lives? Our prickly and protective exterior hides the incredibly beautiful, unique, and surprising qualities inside that are just waiting to be discovered and shared.

Some of the foods that we cover in our articles at the magazine are becoming a lost art, with the wisdom remaining only with the original farmers of the land. I am trying to remedy this and bring light to what they know and do. How to cut a prickly pear, for instance, is no longer something that the general public knows anything about. When I went to my local grocer to ask for help in finding someone to interview, they told me that all their prickly pears arrive already cut and packaged and no one but the island's original farmers knows how to cut them. Wisdom like this cannot go with them when they die. Not a lot of places in the world have prickly pear cactus trees growing, but here in Malta and in Sicily and throughout the Mediterranean, they grow everywhere. Even the giant paddles from which the pears grow have incredible medicinal value and are not being utilized nearly to the degree that they could be. You might recognize the paddles from Latin dishes as *nopales*, which are both edible and considered a vegetable. Now we need to learn how to pick them, slice them, and use them well. Then we need to learn how to pick, pull, cut, and harvest the fruits of the prickly pear.

How to Pull and Cut a Prickly Pear

1. Wear sturdy gloves with a rubber grip so the hairs cannot get inside.
2. Grab the prickly pear fruit with your gloved hand, then twist and pull off the paddles.
3. Place the fruit on a cutting board and slice off the top and bottom of the fruit. (Keep your gloves on while doing all of this.)
4. Make a single slice from the top to the bottom, and from there dig your thumb under and peel the skin off in one full removal.

Once you peel off the skin, you will see the treasure that they have been concealing so well from the outside world. You will find that the pear fruit inside is a bright fuchsia pink, lined with large big black seeds. It's like a disco dance party in its coming out! It looks dyed. It is so bright and so colorful with the hot pink and the black seeds inside. The flavor is simple and just sweet enough. It's like the most incredible dichotomy of context, assumptions, and flavors all rolled into one perfect little secret treasure of fruit.

The prickly pear is any one of us at any given point: beautiful ranges of red, orange, and yellow colors on the outside as the sun seasons it, followed by a hairy and defensive exterior that is much more defiant when touched as opposed to what is seen by the naked eye, followed finally by a deep offering of the most beautiful, subtle, sweet, simple, and yet colorful and wildly surprising inside just waiting to be discovered and let out of its former holding state. Food is life, and the prickly pear is a perfect example of how there is always more than meets the eye.

Food for Thought: Ask Yourself New Questions

Let's redefine our previous questions in a way that will give way to new, bolder answers. We have the basic questions and then we widen our curve a little bit. Again, feel free to write your answers down right here on this very page.

- What would you be trying to do with your life if money was not the only payoff?
- What makes you happy and feel alive when you do it?
- Where would you go if you had unlimited resources?
- What would you do if you had to do something different from what you are doing now?

And lastly, the one question I asked earlier in this chapter:

- What would you do if you were not always so afraid of what could go wrong and instead had the opportunity to have whatever it is you really want come to life?

Food Tip and Recipe

When it comes to Maltese cuisine, one thing you should know is that it has many different influences from the surrounding Mediterranean countries and largely from the Middle East. The Maltese language is 70 percent Arabic, from when the Arabs ruled the land. The two official languages of Malta are Maltese and English. Malta, in a nutshell, has been ruled by the Phoenicians, Greeks, Romans, Arabs, Normans, Aragonese, Habsburg Spain, Knights of St. John, and French, and was under British rule until 1964, when it gained its independence.[5] Many countries in the Middle East ruled Malta at one time or another, so you will find that many flavors and spices come from these places. Malta is a complex mix of so many different territories on this side of the world, and that is reflected in the cuisine.

---

5. Cooper Hewitt, Smithsonian Design Museum, "Malta."

Here is a brief introduction to the spices in the Mediterranean:

- *Greece:* Parsley, oregano, cinnamon, peppermint, bay leaves, marjoram, garlic, onion, nutmeg, salt, fennel, dill, basil, thyme, and a specialty blend of these spices called bokova. In Greek cuisine, it is common to add warm spices like cinnamon and nutmeg to meat sauces. As I'm finding out, in many countries, their own oregano is very important as a spice to them. Greek oregano tastes much stronger (almost like medicine) than the oregano I find in Malta.

- *Spain:* Classic spices include saffron and smoked paprika. Nearby Morocco especially is known to use a spice blend called *ras el hanout*, which has distinct aromas from the cinnamon, lavender, cloves, and rose petals.

- *Malta:* Thyme, oregano, basil.

- *Italy:* Northern, central, and southern Italy are very different regions. However, classic flavors include extra virgin olive oil, oregano, basil, and marjoram.

- *South of France:* Southern France is similar to northern Italy and southern Spain in terms of spices, but it's known more for its creams and butter. It's more about the vegetables than the spices in France.

- *Southern Turkey:* Red pepper flakes, black pepper, sumac, Turkish oregano, allspice, cumin, cinnamon, sesame seeds and nigella seeds, mint, bay leaves, thyme.

- *Middle East:* Baharat is a warm spice blend whose composition depends on whether it's Lebanese, Syrian, Egyptian, Jordanian, Palestinian, Israeli, etc. Each country has its trade secret for the balance of the spices, including cinnamon, cardamom, black pepper, cloves, cumin, nutmeg, coriander, and paprika.

- *Za'atar* is a spice mixture that includes thyme, oregano, and marjoram as the base, plus sumac, toasted sesame seeds, salt, and pepper flakes.

- *Sumac* is a flowering plant that is used in things like hummus, spice rubs, and marinades. It gives a tangy flavor with subtle hints of citrus.

Traditional Maltese Bigilla (Recipe by Daniel Pisani)

Bigilla is an appetizer that tastes wonderful and shows up on every traditional Maltese platter. Think of it like a hummus but with broad beans instead of chickpeas. It is creamy and mild and can be eaten with many things. It is easy to make for yourself. Every recipe I include in this book is designed to be very basic and easy to follow.

On most traditional Maltese appetizer trays (think of a beautiful charcuterie board filled with these items) ordered at any café, you will likely find a small bowl of bigilla in the center, surrounded by fresh olives, capers, Maltese sausages, ġbejniet, sundried tomatoes, butter beans, crackers called *galletti*, and slices of fresh bread with a tomato paste (*kunserva*) already spread on them. A *ġbejna* is a sea salt or heavily peppered cheeselet made of goat milk (naturally fat-free) or sheep's milk (naturally high in fat) or a combination of both, depending on if the cheese is dried or fresh. This is a very traditional and standard appetizer tray offered on this island. It always looks beautiful and is sure to complement just about any meal that is on deck.

This recipe for bigilla can be found in the book *A Plant Based Maltese Kitchen* by Daniel Pisani. He was kind enough to allow me to share it here.

INGREDIENTS

1½ cups (270 grams) dried broad beans or Djerba beans
6½ tablespoons (100 ml) olive oil
½ teaspoon sea salt
5 garlic cloves
Pinch of dried Mediterranean herbs (basil, oregano, and thyme)
1 small fresh chili or ½ teaspoon dried chili
Chopped parsley

DIRECTIONS

Start by soaking the beans in salted water for 12–24 hours.

Prepare a pan with boiling salted water and cook the beans until they are very soft.

Once the beans have cooled down, combine all the ingredients in a food processor, adding more olive oil or water if the consistency is too thick.

Here is a note that is not from the book: Many people add chili flakes to top the dish, along with a drizzle of olive oil and fresh parsley leaves as a garnish.

Marija's Bean and Pasta Soup (Kusksu bil-ful) (Recipe by Ben Muscat)

This is a very common Maltese soup made for lunch or dinner any time of the year. This recipe comes from the Maltese restaurant Ta' Marija. This was Marija's original family recipe, and her son, Ben Muscat, still uses it in their restaurant to this day. He was kind enough to share this family jewel with all of us after he served it to me and I loved it so much. It's simple, hearty, veggie-filled goodness, even more so with the added cheeselet (ġbejna), which kicks up the flavor nicely. The ġbejna looks beautiful upon presentation and tastes really nice with the soup stock.

INGREDIENTS (FOR 6 PEOPLE)

2 tablespoons vegetable oil

1 large onion, finely chopped

1 carrot, cut into rings

1 fresh celery stick, chopped

1 tablespoon tomato paste (kunserva)

1 cup (200 grams) broad beans

1 can polpa (crushed tomatoes)

1 can peas

1 vegetable stock cube

8 cups (2 liters) water

1 cup (250 grams) kuskus (couscous) pasta

Sprinkle of salt and fresh pepper corns

1 teaspoon sugar

Optional for added taste and presentation:
6 cheeselets (ġbejniet), one for each bowl
Freshly grated parmesan cheese

METHOD

In a proper cooking soup bowl, heat 2 tablespoons of vegetable oil. Add the chopped onion, carrot, and celery and brown gently. Stir in the tomato paste, then top up with the beans, crushed tomatoes (polpa), and peas. Dissolve the vegetable stock cube in the water and add to the cooked ingredients. Bring to a boil and add the kuskus (couscous—it's the same thing, only spelled differently, according to location), salt, pepper, and sugar. Keep stirring so the pasta doesn't stick to the bottom. Cook for 15 minutes until the pasta is tender.

PRESENTATION

For a fine presentation of this very typical Maltese dish, you will impress your guests if you put a whole fresh cheeselet (ġbejna) in each soup bowl you are serving. It is always recommended to top the soup with additional freshly grated parmesan cheese.

Chapter 3
Start a Love Affair

A life without a passion project makes for a lackluster dish. What are you passionate about? What makes you come alive? Surrounding yourself with people who are pursuing something and putting themselves out there elevates your own life and helps you attract people who follow the same principles. People meet their best friends and sometimes even fall in love while in medical school, law school, massage school, art school, culinary school, etc. Not only can you find something that you are passionate about, but in finally making the move to go after your passion, you start to attract people into your life who are doing the same. It obviously does not have to be school, but it could be a class or meeting up with a group of people with the same interests. It could be making new friends and asking them to introduce you to things they enjoy. Any number of things can draw you toward a new passion to explore. You cannot just wish to find these people. You have to go out and become the people you are hoping to find. There is always room for more at the table and in your life. Make time to fall in love with a new addition to your life.

You have everything it takes inside you to make something new come to life. Do you believe that? Let's start there. You first have to know that you are both qualified and brave enough to do whatever is calling you. You also have to know that it may or may not turn into something big or significant, but it certainly might. The outcome has the same potential to be one or the other or anywhere in between. But you must trust yourself and understand that taking any steps into someplace or something new will be the reward in and of itself. It is always worth it to learn something new and try something you've never done before. It makes us more confident, stronger, and more resilient. You are not too old and it is not too late. Whatever fun things you wish to add to your life can be made possible in some capacity.

If you are a younger person and just starting to build your own set of skills, know that beginning your practice with the belief that you are fully competent and capable will support the new areas as you allow yourself to explore. This mindset and practice will grow stronger as you go. So many people, when asked what they wish their younger self had known, respond with an answer that revolves around self-confidence in what they didn't realize they were capable of. Many people (myself included) also wish that they would have learned much earlier in life to trust their own internal guidance system above all else. Trust your gut and know that you have everything it takes to manifest your desires into reality.

I'm mostly talking about taking a class or learning a new skill. Start someplace within reach and go from there. We build by taking the steps to achieve our goal. Explore something that you are curious about. If you have dreamed of writing that novel, start writing it now! You do not have to wait to take that class to begin your writing journey; you simply have to write. You do not have to take that class to begin your culinary journey; you can start with new cookbooks and watching videos and then it might lead you to enroll in a class or two and then maybe a full-time school if that is something you dream of doing.

The more important thing to ask yourself is what do you dream of doing? And if you do wish to be doing something more, what in the world has stopped you from doing it? Or has it? I hope you find yourself reading this and thinking to yourself, "What is she talking about? I *am* doing it! I am pursuing my passions and my dreams!" Not every new dream, passion, or goal has to be something you sign up for, but it is something you will absolutely have to show up for. None of this comes true without you!

The Sea and Sky

The Mediterranean Sea has a wholly different energy from any other body of water that I've ever been around. Though I have begun quite a few love affairs while living here, there is none more special or sacred to me than the one I feel with the sea herself. Almost everywhere you go here, you can see her. Almost all roads will lead you to the water's edge. Driving alongside the sea has opened my senses and my soul in a way that I pray I never have to go back to living without. Now that I know what it's like to always live near the water, I can't return to a place without it.

Water has always affected me greatly. So does the moon and its cycles. No matter if you scan your eyes from the sea up to the sky or from the sky down to the sea over here, the colors blend into one another as if they were the same single entity with varying textures. One thing I love about watching the sea is that on some days it's so windy and the sea crashes with waves that fly up so high just up and over the edges of where the water meets the rocks, but if you look farther out toward the middle of the sea, it's perfectly calm. It offers a perspective in real life on how something close up can seem so overwhelming and even disastrous, and yet if you look beyond just the immediate, you can find some clarity. I always remember that on the days when the winds are high and the sea seems angry.

The sky was something my dad taught me about from a young age. He would show me different pictures of the stars and tell me which great philosopher or astronomer had discovered them or named them. Here in the Mediterranean, it feels like we are somehow closer to the moon, closer to the stars and the sun, too. The nearly constant azure blue sky is something that the Mediterranean is known for. Rarely do we see clouds. It's just that beautiful blue color as far and as clear as the eyes can see. The only time the color changes is at sunrise and sunset, when all of a sudden the sky becomes a myriad of bright shades of orange, peach, yellow, and red. Just this morning as I was writing this, I looked out my kitchen door only to see the entire wall covered in a bright orangish peach light from the sun as she announced herself rising up over the sea. Seeing the lights bouncing off the wall, I knew I had to get outside and take a look at the grandeur of the sky this morning. I feel like the more I acknowledge Mother Nature, the more beauty she seems to offer in return. It's a dance, and we are both participating in its intricacies.

There are so many days when the sun rises or sets so brightly that you can almost see the whole box of colors. On any given rainy morning, you may find any number of bright, colorful rainbows across the island and over the sea. Each rainbow presents itself to its people in a way that makes you feel like you are part of the entire universe all raveled into that exact moment. My soul opens up daily from something entirely natural here. When you are up close to so many natural wonders, it's easy to become part of it all with a more appreciative perception.

When I go outside at night and look up at the sky, it looks like I'm standing inside a planetarium. The stars are so bright that it doesn't look real! The sky is so clear almost every night and you can see the constellations everywhere you turn in a full 360. It feels like the moon hangs lower, too. It's always so bright and clear out here. I have made it a nightly habit for many years to sit outside and pray and center myself before going to sleep. I've watched the night sky from the north and south sides of the city back home in Georgia. I've noticed how different the night sky always is when visiting friends in the mountains or along the Gulf Coast of Florida. I am a keen watcher of the night sky. I have always been fascinated with it.

Just this week, I saw three comets fly through the air on the same night. These are things you usually hear about but never seem to be able to see on your own from wherever you are. It is stunning to be in a place where things like this occur without needing a telescope for someone with an untrained eye who just so happens to love to sit outside and watch and wait for possibilities. When the sky lights up and a shooting star shines across or thirty-plus bizarre satellites crawl across the sky, only to find out later that they were satellites from Elon Musk's Starlink project or the comets that NASA had alerted us would be happening all week, it offers you a closer connection to the universe.

Do you know what I love most though? I had no idea that the Starlink satellites were coming. And I didn't know that it was going to be a week of comet activity. And shooting stars are so random that I've only seen two so far. I just happened to be outside when all these things occurred and then found out later what they were. There is always magic happening in the sky, and it seems like over here it's so clear and so close that I can witness it as it happens. This is my personal love affair with the sea and sky, which makes up some of the best parts of my days. It doesn't require any money or sign-up fees. The sky is available to all of us every night in every part of the whole world. It increases my sense of wonder and expands my vision of the enormous number of possibilities that lay beneath it. It is a simple act, making time to sit outside at night and observe the sky above, but it is so worth it to me. Maybe my offering this to you as a practice, a devotion, can in some small way help you to realize that you, too, are a sacred and specific part of this very big world and that the possibilities that lay beneath that very same sky apply just as much to you as they do to me.

Being this close to the natural world helps me to be more aware of my surroundings and give thanks more often. It helps to ground me and center my body and clear my mind. The sea opens me up and makes me feel comforted by the vastness of never seeing the end of it. The sky reminds me that while there are limits, I cannot find them because it is too expansive to limit my vision. There are many times when it's hard to see where the sea ends and the sky begins. Even on gray days, the sea looks gray. On bright blue days, it looks like lines of different shades of blue from bottom to top. Whether you start by looking up at the sky and going down or looking at the water and going up, they match. All the colors match and blend into one another. I've never seen that while looking at other bodies of water. It is indescribable unless you can see it for yourself. The Mediterranean Sea has a magic all her own.

The Fisherman and the Sea

There are two types of fishermen here in Malta. The first are those who go out to sea in a small boat (the traditional boat native to Malta is called a luzzu) every morning before the crack of dawn to catch the fish that swim closer to port. They catch their fish with the line and a bucket using smaller fish to lure them in. It is an art form and requires years of learning and practice. This type of fishing is handed down from generation to generation. The second are those who go out to sea for days at a time in a group in a larger fishing boat and catch their fish in much larger nets. Either way, in order to commit yourself to being a lifelong fisherman, it is a love affair that you choose to take on or you don't. Here, if you choose not to be a fisherman, you can easily still work in the family business and run the fish market where the fish are sold. You can open a restaurant that serves fish or some other type of related business.

There is a restaurant called Fins & Gills located not near the fishing village but instead on the other side of the island that wins awards every year for its fish and chips and has only five things on the menu, all fish dishes. Almost all the fish they serve is caught by the owner's mother each day. She goes out every morning and catches the fish herself and takes them to her son's restaurant, where you walk up and order and take it to go. It is a tiny little fish place and one that we frequent often. She takes the other fish to her own fish market, where the locals buy from her. Everyone knows her and loves her and knows that the fish they are buying came out of the sea just hours earlier.

The lone fisherman, Venunzio, whom I interviewed in Marsaxlokk, goes out to sea on his boat every morning at 3:30 a.m. to catch fish to sell at the markets that morning. People who buy the fish wake up extra early to get their seafood within just a few hours of it being caught, because they know it will all be gone by mid-morning. This is where the family business is paramount to the lone fisherman's ability to stay in business. The fisherman goes out all night and comes back to the edge of port before dawn, where some of his children are waiting to take the fish inside and straighten them out and get them on ice. When I say straighten them out, I do not mean to clean them, but to put them on ice. The fish are in whatever position they were in when they were caught, so the fisherman's children take each fish from the cooler and straighten out the body and place it in an icebox. Then they line up the fish against each other, with one head facing one tail and the next tail facing the next head, so the ice can get between each fish body and keep them all frozen and fresh by covering the most surface area of the fish. From there, they either put the fish in freezers or run them to the fish markets to put out on trays that very morning. The fishing village here in Malta is something to see, with all the different covered tents housing tray upon tray of freshly caught fish from that morning. An incredible array of the various fish lines both sides of the aisle, depending on what each fisherman was able to catch that day and what type of boat and process they used to get them.

The fish market is loud and insanely crowded with people from all over the world coming off the cruise ships and tour buses to see all the seafood. You will find octopus, clams, sea bass, mackerel, lampuki (baby mahi-mahi), squid, shrimp, crabs, and so many more lined up tray by tray, with the people in charge of each tent yelling out something to try to get your attention. It is pure madness! It is also a daily affair, especially on Sundays, starting early in the morning.

Every day you will see tour buses pull up and crowds of people get off to go see the famous fishing village. To them, it's a show in and of itself and a great place to shop for fish. There are also many flea markets that line the streets, carrying anything from toys to purses and hats, pajamas, lace tablecloths, spices, salts, oils, and an array of wildly colored cream-filled cannoli and nougats. For the fishermen and their families, this is their daily life. This is their love affair. It is all family, all fishing, all the time. People who live there have been there all their lives. They wouldn't dream of being anyplace else, or at least the people I've talked to feel that way. There is a great sense of pride in their family business, and they all take care of one another. They do not grow up and move away.

They grow up and have children and start them young learning all they can about the inheritance of their family's legacy.

When a fisherman gets off the boat, he goes to bed for the day to be able to get up later and do it all again. Everyone has a part to play and it must be done every single day. There are no weekends off or vacation days. There might be one or two holidays where they don't fish, but that's only because everyone is at home with their families and no one is buying from the fresh markets on those days. Their vacation days come on stormy days when the winds are too high to go out to sea. Their lives are dictated strictly by the weather from day to day.

When you get far from the natural world of sun, sky, sea, and wind, these things don't come to mind so much. But to the people on this tiny island, where everyone lends a hand in our feeding and growing, it is everything. Mother Nature has a starring role in life here. She regulates everything we see, do, and eat. It can be exhausting, dirty, and incredibly hard work. At the same time, it can be utterly glorious to our bodies and souls. I've never met more grateful and content people than those in that fishing village. To me, this is where the energy of Malta can be felt the strongest. Going down to the fishing village as many times as I have, especially after what it took for me to land my lampuki interview, I do not take these friends for granted in the least. They are a very tight-knit group, and to be welcomed in at every visit is something very special to me. Learning from the fishermen and their families has been a treasure.

There are benches every few feet all along the water's edge of the village where anyone can sit down and admire the many boats floating steadily by. The lineup of luzzu boats in bright shades of blue, green, red, and yellow, all arranged in various orders, never missing any of the four colors, and all of them with the evil eye on both sides to protect them as they set out to sea, is something so beautiful it is beyond description. Sitting out there and admiring the beauty has become a new and beloved affair for my heart. I still believe that the heart of the island of Malta beats straight out of the fishing village.

Going Back to What You Loved

By living here, I have had a change in perspective on the idea that in order to rediscover some happiness you might want to go back to doing something you once loved. I learned this because in this big move, I thought I would go back to practicing tai chi with all new people. I retired many years ago after my original teacher stopped teaching, and with every attempt it became more difficult for me to find my passion in the practice.

I thought that with moving here, I could start over and it would be my tai chi practice again the way it once was. I took one class in a sweaty boxing gym and realized that (1) I didn't want to practice indoors and (2) it didn't fit with who I was anymore. As much as I'd love to return to how it felt to me back when it was my passion, it simply is not a part of the new person I have spent years creating in the aftermath of letting it go in the first place. Tai chi is not a pathway to finding my groove again. It is not the door to the house where my new passion will be found. I have been many different people throughout my life. With each new practice, I have thrown myself into it deeply and entirely. And with each end came a new beginning into something else, though not immediately. This is how I have been able to explore myself so well. I go all in. I also take the necessary time to mourn the loss when my time in a practice comes to a close and I must find a new path with a new focus.

People often suggest going back to what you used to love as an option for finding passion or healing or to fill any sort of void. The truth is, you left that something behind for a reason, and depending on that reason, it may or may not be the pathway to find passion again in your life. When I was younger I loved gymnastics. That led to cheerleading, which I did through college. There was no place else to go after that, and so it was over. It was a hard stop and had run its course. It was painful for me to leave them both behind, and I felt lost for a long time trying to find something else to focus on and put my self-identity into. I will miss them always. They are simply not sports that you can continue to grow into, but they can open you up to other practices, such as yoga or dance, that will help you maintain some of the movements and practices.

My friend and personal trainer here in Malta is hitting the age where he is retiring from playing professional football (known as soccer in the United States) and is moving into full-time coaching. It has been a tough transition for him. It always is. He could always play on a recreational team, of course, but it will never be the glory days again that he has built his entire life around. He is currently teaching at the sports academy here on the island and coaching for a lead team as well, but nothing feels like it does when it is you out there on the field. I understand this so well. Sports are a really hard thing to walk away from, because they bring us so much inner joy and excitement and discipline and there is nothing that compares to it…until you find something entirely new that feeds your soul in a way that is different yet enough to satiate your appetite.

Some people pick up kayaking or whitewater rafting. I know someone who started skydiving at age thirty-five and joined a team where they did all sorts of crazy stunts out of the airplane. My mentor and professor for both undergraduate and graduate schools took up ballroom dancing in his sixties. He went through years of going to the gym and trying step aerobics and anything else to keep him fit, but nothing made him nearly as happy as football. When he took to the ballroom, he transformed into something totally new and adventurous. He keeps winning medals and traveling around with his dance partner and sharing all that he is doing with those of us who love to watch him. He continues to inspire us all so much. It was not easy for him to find something he loves so much and it certainly did not happen immediately, but it did happen and he is completely committed to his new way of life.

Each of us is the phoenix rising in the world. We rise from the ashes of something that was potentially catastrophic in our lives and emerge stronger, smarter, and more capable than ever. While none of us can ever be the same person we were back then, do not ever sell yourself short by believing that the passion you had at one time will never be matched or even surpassed by an entirely new version of you, because it certainly can. It just won't show up wearing the same clothes. You will still be able to recognize your igniting inner excitement, because you know it so intimately. When that light comes on again, move toward it all the way. Throw yourself into the deep. You deserve to be happy and filled with excitement for whatever opportunities may come into your life.

Let's look at Dr. Bernie Siegel's story of his patient who put down the violin because his parents made him. For this man, going back to playing reawakened his soul to such a level that he skipped his grim cancer prognosis and flew up from the ashes while playing his beloved violin and joining the local orchestra. Then there was the patient who moved to a place in Colorado that he considered to be the most beautiful. It was a place he had only dreamed of moving to before he was sick, but he finally allowed himself to live there, sincerely and freely. That is what saved him. It gave him new life.

Passion can be found again. Where you find yours will probably not be in the same place that any of the rest of us find ours. It is a soulful and independent path. Trust that and follow it all the way in. You are not without desire. None of us is. Listen to that still small voice, that flicker of burning passion that has been hidden deep within. Recognize it for what it is and follow it wherever it may lead. Let it introduce itself to you without fear of being shut down or dismissed as something silly. Silly is a spice we could enjoy more often, too.

Finding a love affair in your life does not happen in only one direction. You might go back in time. How many people, through social media or even a school reunion, have found their old high school sweetheart after they divorced or their spouse passed away and found love again? This happens more often than you might think! The past certainly can hold certain keys to our passion and pleasure, but it is not always in a lockbox waiting to be rediscovered. You are allowed to start again and create something entirely new for yourself and your precious life. Cul-de-sacs are often built on dead-end roads for a reason!

You can turn around and go in another direction to find the right avenue of expression for yourself and your passion. It does not have to become a career or a relationship. It's just something to elevate your life with the same vigor that we elevate our cooking by knowing how and when to add those spices. It's the time right now to add another spice to your dish! What is that spice you've been looking for lately? Where has it been hiding? In a new location? In the cabinet? Has it been waiting to be in season again? What is it? Or is there anything you are missing right now in the dish that sits in front of you that could make your life taste just a little bit zestier? And if you found that spice right now, would you add it to your life?

You get to be the cook in this kitchen. Your new spice could be something simple such as journaling or meditation or singing karaoke! It doesn't have to have a big price tag attached to it and it doesn't need an entry fee. It is entirely up to you to decide what would add just the right extra seasoning to your life to make your dish go from mundane to whimsical. It also doesn't have to be a big move or even a new daily habit. It could be a weekly or even monthly class or practice. You get to choose how you play this part of the game. You just have to be willing to begin to ask yourself the questions with answers that lead to new directions.

What Makes You Curious?

I loved taking the course on spicing up salads and main course dishes at the Mediterranean Culinary Academy. I plan to do more of that and more of the interviews I'm getting to do with the local farmers for the magazine. Truth be told, I'd love to just go sit in the kitchens of other people's homes and watch what they do there for meals. Every time I'm in someone's home, they are making something that I've not seen before. Much of the time they are basic meals that look amazing. I don't know how to make those simple staples yet, but I want to learn.

Soup and bread are big staples here, and there are tons of soups they make from season to season. I've always associated soup with two things: (1) winter and (2) being sick. Here, soup is on the table all the time. They say it's an easy way to get your vegetables. I want to learn all the tricks of the trade here and soak up everything I can learn from all the people who have moved here from surrounding countries as well. I have become passionately curious about people. *These* people. All of them. I want to sit down with anyone who wants to have a conversation, especially if they can cook while they're at it!

My level of curiosity has become bigger than I can contain. It has turned itself into an actual project, and I am following it down every single road I possibly can to bring that passion to the table. I love the people here. I love knowing where they came from and what makes them happy. I love that my Greek friends have food for literally everything you need. If you are sick, they have the *only thing that you should eat*. If you are celebrating, they have several foods that you should eat. I love that their lunchtime is something to celebrate daily, and it is done so through their foods. The food all around the Mediterranean is the entire culture's love language, and it is spoken clearly and tastes overwhelmingly delicious.

I love that these countries have foods for all occasions that are only made once a year, coupled with drinks to boot. Because there is always a new season of growth and a new month of saints to celebrate in Malta, Italy, and Spain, the foods that quickly go out of season are fast replaced with something else we might love. It gives us something to be both grateful for and excited about. People here drink more often or at least more freely, but not so freely that you find them falling down in the streets.

I find myself more relaxed over here. The people in these Mediterranean cultures are very boisterous in general. They talk with their hands, and they speak loudly and with animation. These are my people. I have always been accused of being too loud. Here I'm not too loud and I'm not too animated. I fit in just right. I'm like the Goldilocks of the Maltese! I like who I am becoming over here better than who I used to be. I like the process I'm going through of integrating who I have been before with who I am becoming now. My vision of life itself has become so much clearer. So many things that I used to get caught up in before seem so trivial to me now.

Being here has changed me as a person in a great many ways. It has humbled me and opened me up and taught me different values and encouraged me to ask myself more questions about everything. Being in different surroundings will change anyone. That's why I want so much for you who are reading this to realize that if there are parts of your life that are not nourishing to your soul, you can change the narrative by changing the surroundings you are in. It doesn't necessarily mean moving to a new location, but if you are not happy, it does ask that you consider moving outside of whatever current situation might be making it that way. It is possible but not necessarily easy. Of course, the things in life that are worth doing are rarely easy.

Make It Your Own

There are many ways to begin a love affair. It doesn't have to have anything to do with other people, but more than likely whenever you do put yourself into something new, your chances heighten significantly of meeting people who are also putting themselves into something new. We make new kinds of friendships or even sometimes romantic partnerships with other people who share our interests and curiosities, but that's just a bonus of creating a new outlet for your curiosity. I encourage everyone to always have something in their lives that they feel passionate about. I feel it is an important part of living a well-balanced life. Too many times we put passion on the back burner in pursuit of work, chores, have-to-dos, and not-want-to-dos. But even the hardest workers and the most disciplined people still need a little hideaway in pursuit of a purpose that is all their own.

Here in this very different culture in Malta, the pursuit of a personal passion is not something that people need to be reminded of or taught. It's passed down through their genetic code to work hard and play just as hard, and to not feel bad or guilty when you are sticking to just one of those. They are not out doing something fun while thinking of all the other things they *should be* doing. On warm sunny days, they cut out early from the office and get into the water every chance they get, and they don't feel bad about it. Many locals keep swimsuits and swim gear in their cars. Some even do a sea swim during their lunch hour before heading back to the office. The locals especially never stay far from the sea.

Here in Malta, the arts are also much more highly encouraged. There is always some sort of art or music event. There are classes for everything if you want to learn a new skill and not just watch other people perform. There are baking schools and gardening schools all over this island, as well as a school of performing arts. The level of appreciation for the finer things in life is evident everywhere you look. It's an appreciation of a richer culture that is less focused on the money side of things. The people here tend to be more focused on the deeper and internally fulfilling side of being rich.

Food for Thought: Decide What Feeds Your Soul

After I moved here, I made the decision that I no longer want to do things that do not feed my soul. If it doesn't bring me joy, I don't want to keep showing up for it. I will do what needs to be done and I will do so with a smile, but if it does not feed me down deep, I'm not going to be a repeat customer in any venue. There are so many things to go and find and chase down that might be more exhilarating, and I want more of that. It's like eating the same breakfast of Cream of Wheat without salt or sugar when you could be eating a bowl of Greek yogurt peanut butter oatmeal delight. They are both still breakfast, but one leaves me feeling that much more satisfied as I start my day. Ask yourself these questions:

- If you could begin a whole new love affair or passion project, what would your new creative refuge look like? Is it something you have access to in your daily life?
- If you could learn something completely new, what would it be?
- Is there any part of your life that feels out of balance or missing somehow? If so, is there anything you can do to transform it into something tangible?
- Are you willing to put yourself out there into something braver, bolder, and spicier simply for the sake of elevating your own

life? What would that be? If you have an answer to this question, then I must ask, are you doing something about it?

Food Tip and Recipe

Greek Yogurt Peanut Butter Oatmeal Delight (Recipe by Emily Francis)

This is a recipe I put together simply based on what I like here in the Mediterranean and how it makes me feel when I start my day this way. I never thought before to add peanut butter to my yogurt, but it is a lovely combination for children and adults alike. If you have not mixed Greek yogurt with peanut butter or almond butter and oats, it's delicious. You can make a bowl of nutritional decadence by combining the following ingredients.

INGREDIENTS

A hefty spoonful of peanut butter, almond butter, or the nut butter of
    your choice
Rolled oats (uncooked) to your preferred consistency
Bananas and/or fresh berries
Chia seeds, flax seeds, and/or hemp seeds
A drizzle of local honey

DIRECTIONS

With this recipe, you have a perfectly balanced, healthy way to start your day. You can also make overnight oats with the same ingredients, but check the recipe for the addition of coconut or almond milk. Check the labels of your Greek yogurt. What they sell locally to me in Malta is imported from Greece. The brands sold here are not sold in the United States, where higher sugar and chemical contents are usually found. As I look at my container of Greek yogurt sitting in my fridge, the ingredients are pasteurized skimmed cow's milk, pasteurized skimmed concentrated cow's milk, milk cream, milk proteins, yogurt culture. Notice that there is no sugar in it. Now I offer the ingredient list of a well-known brand of Greek yogurt in the United States so you can make your own comparison: cultured grade-A non-fat milk, water, fructose, contains less than 1% of modified corn starch, natural and artificial flavors, sucralose, citric acid, potassium sorbate (to maintain freshness), acesulfame potassium, sodium citrate.

The health benefits of eating Greek yogurt fully depend on which brand of yogurt you are eating. It goes so far beyond any single ingredient, too. Eating naturally and locally sourced food is one of the greatest gifts we can all receive for our health and wellbeing. People often complain about the quality of the food wherever they live in the world. I still find that here sometimes, but never from the farmers. They grow food that they are very proud of and they go to tremendous lengths to keep the soil and the plants healthy and pesticide-free. I think this is a huge contributing factor to having so many elderly people here and in countries that border the Mediterranean. It's the weather and lifestyle too, but it's largely due to the quality of the soil and therefore the quality of the food without a doubt.

Greek Remedies

Even though these recipes are not for delight, they might be something you'll want to keep on hand for the next time you get sick. I offer them here as a gift from my Greek friends and hope you won't ever need to use them! I wanted to offer these remedies for illness because the people here are very serious about what should and should not be eaten when our bodies become unbalanced.

Greek Remedy for a Stomach Bug
(Ingredient list by Loukia Makou)

Arborio rice

Lemon

Salt

Olive oil

Greek Remedy for a Cold or Flu (Avgolemono Soup) (Recipe by Loukia Makou)

This Greek soup is often referred to as Greek penicillin.

INGREDIENTS

1 large free-range chicken

1 carrot

1 onion

1 celery stalk

1 cup (100 grams) rice or orzo pasta

Salt and pepper

EGG LEMON SAUCE

2 eggs

2 lemons

METHOD: CHICKEN SOUP

Put the chicken in a large pot. Add the vegetables. Cover with water and bring to a boil. If any foam or chicken bits rise to the top, remove and discard them. Once boiling, reduce the temperature to medium and cook for 90 minutes until the chicken is tender.

Drain the stock into a small pot. Add the rice or orzo and boil the soup on low heat until the rice or orzo is cooked. Add salt and pepper and remove from heat.

METHOD: EGG LEMON SAUCE (AVGOLEMONO)

This is the part that makes the chicken soup into something magical and even more healing.

Beat the two eggs thoroughly and add the juice from two freshly squeezed lemons. Using bottled lemon juice won't give as strong of an effect, so try to stick to juicing fresh lemons.

Pour the sauce over the chicken soup and thicken over low heat for a few minutes.

Some people separate the egg yolks from the whites. They whisk the whites and then add in the yolks, but this is not entirely necessary. Beating the eggs together is easier and serves the same purpose.

Chapter 4

Always Salt

In the cooking class I took here, one of the things the instructor, Chef Ariel Guivisdalsky, kept saying was, "Always salt." Salt brings out the flavors of everything else in the dish. He says: "You don't add salt for a salty flavor. You add salt to help the foods release their natural liquids. The natural flavors become concentrated and more enhanced because of the small addition of salt." He continues: "Salt, just like sugar, enhances the flavors. If you are trying to get a sweet dish, you need a pinch of salt to highlight the flavor of the sweet sugar. Likewise, to taste the salt flavor in a dish, you need a pinch of sugar. Salt encourages the food to release its natural flavors."

When it comes to salt, you can always add, but you cannot subtract. You go slow with salt and handle it with care. You add just a small amount, layer by layer and pinch by pinch. Once you put in too much, the dish is ruined and you cannot pull it back out. This applies to so many things in life. So many times in life we need to go in increments in order to put in just the right amount of ourselves to unlock our potential flavor and create our best dish with what we've got. We go slowly, steadily, and surely, adding each effort in layer by layer, pinch by pinch, instead of dumping in the whole box or going in blindly, not really realizing what we are getting ourselves into.

Salt can ruin any dish when it's too strong, and it can leave a dish lackluster when it isn't included. It elevates all the flavors and turns them into something new. Salt is the central character of any dish whether savory or even sweet, maximizing the flavor. It can play small or it can play big. But in the end, in every dish and all of life…always salt.

Salt is more than something to bring flavor to a dish. There are many ways to use salt, from old superstitions to detox cleansing agents to understanding the different types of salt and the purpose of each. In my experience as a bodyworker, salt has meant a great deal to me for clearing and grounding. It also pulls out the toxins from the body when added to a bath. A detox bath with both sea salt and Epsom salt has been my go-to for fighting illness and following any massage, chiropractic, or acupuncture treatment in which the energy will get moving and you need an exit point from the body to release the acids from your whole being. My children have been taking salt baths since they were babies. I love to wash my face while taking a salt bath. I will introduce you to the many ways salt can be used and which types are best to work with in each scenario. Even though we categorize salt as sodium chloride and tend to leave it under that title, salts are not the same and vary widely in the kitchen as well as everywhere else.

Cooking Salt: Table, Kosher, Sea, or Himalayan

There are many types of salt. Some you can cook with, while others you should never cook with, such as Epsom salt or sea salt from the Dead Sea. These are not used in the kitchen but have very distinct uses in other areas of our lives for well-being. Each type of salt has its own distinct personality, and we pair them according to their purpose.

Table Salt

Table salt, or sodium chloride, is mined from salt deposits, processed into small crystals, and then stripped of its nutrients of magnesium, calcium, and potassium by way of manufacturing. Iodine is then added, which is the major benefit of ingesting table salt rather than sea salt. Iodine is a necessary nutrient for thyroid hormone production. Table salt, or sodium, as it is labeled on foods, is in basically every food that comes in a box. It's everywhere. Do not worry about getting enough iodine unless you are eating an incredibly strict diet only from home and don't manage to get iodine through any other source. Research has been shown that people in Europe do carry a risk of lower iodine levels because they don't use the amounts of salt in their baked goods and dairy products that are used commercially in countries such as the US.[6]

Kosher Salt

Kosher salt is a favorite of many chefs because of its larger crystals. It is often used to tenderize meats. It is still heavily processed and not as naturally untouched as it would be had it come directly evaporated from the sea. Kosher salt is not iodized.

Sea Salt

Sea salt from natural sea sources occurs in many places around the world, including France, England, Iceland, Pakistan, Hawaii, and the Mediterranean for starters. Sea salt for cooking is considered healthier due to its natural source of sodium along with the added benefits of minerals that come from the sea and are not stripped away with any processing. Sea salt is evaporated from the sea and not extracted the way table salt is in mines.

Sea salt comes with an array of necessary minerals known as trace minerals that are important factors in a healthy diet. Sea salt naturally contains magnesium, calcium, iron, and potassium. A grain of sea salt is slightly larger than that of table salt, even if they are both finely or coarsely ground. Sea salts are not iodized and remain in their natural state or as close to it as possible. Coarse sea salt is the most common salt used by chefs because of its crunchy texture and more pronounced taste. Other than the grains being larger (so we use less of it), the coarse variety is the same thing, just not ground down into a fine texture. Sea salt also varies according to which sea it is from. This may change the taste and

---

6. Leonard, "Does Pink Himalayan Salt Have Any Health Benefits? Risks and Considerations."

texture, but sea salt from any natural place is both the more natural and the healthier option when used in small amounts.

Himalayan Pink Salt

Himalayan pink salt is a sea salt found in the foothills of the Himalayas, specifically in the Punjab province of Pakistan. It carries the same sodium percentage as table salt, as well as the same healthier trace minerals and value as sea salt from other areas such as the Mediterranean. Pink sea salt, or Himalayan sea salt, adds great value to a dish and can help with hydration when pinched into a liquid. Instead of drinking electrolyte drinks, which have added dyes and chemicals, I often drink grapefruit juice diluted by half with water and a pinch of pink sea salt to allow my body to hold on to the water a bit more effectively.

Himalayan pink salt is considered a healthier version, much the same way that sea salt is categorized. The difference is in the locations where the salt is harvested. Each land offers a specific set of blessings in its food, and this is one primary example. If choosing between Himalayan salt or Mediterranean Sea salt, know that they are both great choices to cook with. I liken it to finding local honey, in that you might choose the one that is most local to you.[7]

Healing Salt

Salt adds an earthy element of grounding, cleaning, and clearing. Spilled salt is associated with treachery and lies, and throwing a pinch of salt over your shoulder has been a very long-standing tradition to ward off evil. In Mahayana Buddhist traditions, they use salt to ward off evil spirits. Salt is thrown over the left shoulder to prevent evil from entering their homes after attending a funeral.[8] In Christian tradition, two superstitions are based on da Vinci's painting of the Last Supper: never seat thirteen at a dinner table and spilling salt brings bad luck. In the painting itself, a container of spilled salt sits next to Judas's elbow. This brings

---

7. Leonard, "Does Pink Himalayan Salt Have Any Health Benefits?"
8. EricT_CulinaryLore, "Spilling Salt Is Bad Luck and Other Salt Superstitions."

an association of bad luck, treachery, and lies. In this tradition, "people throw a pinch of salt over their left shoulder to blind the devil waiting there."[9]

It seems to be confirmed that the practice of providing protection by throwing salt is done with the right hand pinching the salt and throwing it over the left shoulder. According to superstition not related to any specific religion, the devil stands behind your left shoulder waiting to find a way in. You may find people sitting down at a restaurant who quickly throw salt over their shoulder to be sure that they are safe and protected before they begin enjoying the delights of the foods being served. Some do it as sort of a preemptive strike against any evil just in case. Others do it after salt has been spilled or something else comes along that makes them believe they need to utilize a sort of clearing technique to undo any bad luck that might have been unleashed upon them.

Epsom Salt

Epsom salt is something quite different from other types of salt. It is no longer found in the original location of Epsom, England, or if it is, there is no longer enough of it to generate a viable business of selling it. These days, Epsom salts for the most part are created in a lab, and its scientific properties vary greatly from those of both sea salt and table salt. No matter how a type of salt comes to be, it serves a specific purpose and elevates anything it touches into something that could not have existed quite the same way without it. Note that Epsom salts are not to be eaten, but rather are used for muscle aches or as a suppository to move the bowels.

To Protect Your Space

To create a higher-vibrational space for protection, creativity, and health, there is a practice we can do using salt as one of the four elements: fire, air, earth, and water. For earth, the item used would be salt (sea salt preferred). For fire, it would be a lit candle. For air, it would be a stick of incense, and for water, it would be a holy water or water infused with

---

9. Hedley-Dent, "So Why Do We Throw Salt over Our Shoulder?"

stones or anything else that elevates the water for healing. To create the space, begin by cleaning the room in which the items representing the elements will be placed. Next, place each item in a glass bowl in one corner of the room until all four corners have an element in them. This is a simple yet powerful way to use the forces of nature to cleanse your personal or professional space.

Salt from the Dead Sea

I spent a great many years ordering bags of bulk sea salt from the Dead Sea to create salt bath jars to sell and give as gifts to clients. Sea salt from the Dead Sea is used more for its therapeutic benefits to the body and face. Cleopatra was known to go to great lengths to secure the salt from the Dead Sea for her beauty treatments and face washing.[10] Salt from the Dead Sea is much too bitter to use in the kitchen, but it does have tremendous healing properties for the skin.

A blend of sea salt and Epsom salt tends to have the best of both worlds in terms of therapeutic benefits. The muscle relaxer components of Epsom salts and the detoxifying elements of the sea salt to pull out the toxins that need to be removed from the body following treatments combine to form an effective blend. Never once in those years of ordering that salt did I stop to think about where it came from beyond wanting it to be from the Dead Sea. I never considered who handled it, how it came to be, and the incredible perfection that must have been required to harvest and collect the salt itself. These are things that are so easy to take for granted unless you have the opportunity to meet people who do it for a living. The entire process from start to finish to bring the salts into your hands is laborious.

Salt Pans of the Mediterranean

The sea salt that we can get here in the Mediterranean is used for therapeutic treatments as well as in the kitchen. Salt from the Mediterranean Sea has a crunchy texture and tremendous flavor. I had the privilege of

---

10. The Salt Box, "Dead Sea Salt: The Ultimate Guide to Uses, Origins, Benefits."

meeting and interviewing a woman named Josephine and her parents (the Cini family), who produce salt pans through their family business, Xwejni Salt Pans by Leli tal-Melh. Josephine grew up harvesting the family's sea salt. The pans have been in their family since the 1800s and were featured in season 1 of the Netflix series *Restaurants on the Edge*.[11] During our time together, Josephine explained that there are only three ingredients needed to make sea salt. (Here we go again with the perfect trilogy of creating something natural and to perfection!) As I list the ingredients, they will sound so simple, but as we know, it's never as simple as it seems.

There are salt pans all around the islands that do not hold enough salt at any given time to be able to harvest it. Salt pans are very large squares of salt embedded in the rock that borders the sea. There are usually many squares of these salt pans, and it looks like a giant checkerboard sitting along the water's edge or just above. There are a lot of ghost town salt pans here, and they are a sad sight to behold. Why? Because it takes exactly these three ingredients in exactly the right amounts to make the sea salt come to life and process it to the point that it makes it out of the pans and onto our tables. These are the three ingredients needed to make sea salt:

- The sun
- The wind
- The sea

Simple, right? Wrong. If the winds are off or too strong, the salt does not come in, or it comes in briefly and then is carried away as the sea recedes. If the sun is not shining directly into the pans, the salt is not able to be dried of all the excess moisture that the sea carries. If the sea herself does not come up and deposit her treasure into the flats, into the flat part of each square of the pan itself, then it will not be there at all to harvest. Sometimes the wind is too rough, and as Josephine explains, "Sometimes

---

11. Xuereb, "Restaurants on the Edge by Netflix."

nature wants it back." When the winds are too rough and they come in from the north, the salt dries rougher and more flaky even though it carries the same flavor.[12] Here in Malta, the north winds come from Sicily, while the south winds come from Africa, from the desert. You can determine the direction of the wind by the color of the rain that falls, because the African desert brings brown rain from the sand and debris from the desert, and the cars are covered in brown almost instantly.

Every harvest of salt is different depending on the level of the winds. The sun, the wind, and the sea have to work together in perfect unison to create a harmonious blend that we would want to taste and use in our dishes. Now that I regularly visit Gozo (the sister island of Malta that we travel to by ferry) for the exact purpose of buying my salt from the Cini family, I can taste the difference between their sea salt and any other salt I buy. Other sellers have even tried to pass off counterfeit salt (and other products such as olive oils) as though it were the same product (with the caveat that the salt might have remnants of nuts or other allergens from processing). The real Cini family salt has no such mixing. The salt goes from the salt pans, through their own hands, and into the bags to sell. I know exactly whose hands this salt has passed through. The grains of the salt are never ground into a fine salt, either. This salt is served as either coarse salt or salt flakes, and that is solely dependent on the level of the winds that are helping to develop the salt itself from day to day and month to month.

The Cini family harvests the salts every Monday and Thursday during the warmer months. They harvest on one side of the pans and then the other, meaning the pans to the left or the right side of the dividing line. Imagine a giant checkerboard of squares, each with a flat center. The set of salt pans, or squares, is then divided by a rope or other line to delineate one group of squares and then another. They have a Monday side of the salt pans and a Thursday side of the salt pans. The two sides are never harvested on the same day, as each has its own specific time of apprecia-

---

12. Emily in Malta, "Emily in Malta: Gozitan Sea Salt."

tion by the sun to dry out the salt crystals from the excess water. Something so simple requires such amazing precision to bring it to life, and there are so few people left in the world who are willing to do it. Their work begins at 4:00 a.m. on those harvest days. They have twelve large pools that they fill with water through a large hose and 350 small pans where they extract the salt. The hose has a filter inside it, so that as the seawater moves through the tube and into the pools, any plastics or trash will be caught and filtered.

When walking around the salt pans, you can step only on the sides, never in the actual pans. Josephine says that the small pans are like the "kitchen table," so you have to be extremely careful in the handling of the salt there. Then they brush the salt into a small mound in the center of each pan. From there, they use a brush and a pan to collect the salt from the small pans and place it into individual buckets. Then they have a large bar that they place across their backs, with a bucket attached to each side of the bar by a long chain. They walk evenly, holding two buckets filled with salt to a larger area where the small swept-up salt hills now form one gigantic hill of salt. They place a tarp over this hill and large stones around the edges to allow the sun to evaporate all the water from the salt before they divide and package it.

They begin their morning harvest at 4:00 a.m. and have to be finished by 7:00 a.m. or the heat will be too much to be able to work in. Once the water has evaporated, they place the salt directly into the bags for sale at their shop located just across the road from the water. Josephine's parents have two chairs sitting just outside the shop door, and they sit there from open to close to greet customers and fill the orders. They have been together for over fifty-two years. Josephine has been working with her father harvesting salt since she was four years old.

Sunshine and Sea Salt

When it comes to the way the salt feels in the Mediterranean Sea, it is something different from what I have experienced when tasting and touching salt in the oceans. When I get into the water here in Malta, the salt feels lighter, softer even, but it also feels like it is not going to leave you. It stays with you long after you get out of the water. It stays on your skin and the taste stays in your mouth. The sand is completely different here too. It has thicker granules than anything I've ever seen in the Gulf or by the ocean in the United States and the Caribbean. The sand here is not something I can even liken to the sand in any other part of the world. It is really hard to get off even after a shower. The sand and the salt here almost form a sticky paste against your skin. They somehow like to team up and work together to stick around long after your day at the beach has ended. I like it, though. It has its own personality that way. It lets me know I am not anyplace I have ever been before, and that feels sticky yet exhilarating all at the same time.

The Salt in Me Honors the Salt in You

A dish without salt or a world without you specifically in it would never be able to reach any real level of delight. You are a very specific and exact part of this universe, and the world would not look, feel, or taste the same without you in it. You must understand your value. Salt is a tricky little thing that requires just the right touch. Salt is the exact flavor that it brings. You know what you are getting when it comes to salt. You might be a bit salty yourself. We can all be a lot or even too much for some people. Remember, though, those are not your people.

Some foods taste too salty and we grimace as we quickly push them away. Some are so plain that we have to grab that salt shaker and shake some sense into it. Learning to find a balance within yourself will go a long way. Be exactly who you are; make no excuses or claims. Just show up little by little and layer by layer and discover the brilliance that you can express in your elevation of both life and love. I see you. I see your worth. And I see me and I recognize my worth. Together we can spice up a heck of a dish. Always salt. Always you. And always me.

Food for Thought: What Are Your Three?

If it's the trilogy of the sun, the wind, and the sea that makes for the perfect sea salt, what are the three keywords that you would say make up the best version of you?

1.

2.

3.

Food Tip and Recipe

Because adding a salt recipe for a food tip seems unnecessary, I thought I would offer my simple recipe for a solid detox bath using both the Epsom salt and the sea salt of your choice. A detox bath is something that can be very useful at the onset of not feeling well, after any sort of body treatment such as massage, chiropractic, or acupuncture, or at the start of a new season when the weather changes abruptly and you need to help your body balance itself.

Sea Salt and Epsom Salt Detox Bath
(Recipe by Emily Francis)

INGREDIENTS

1–2 cups (225–450 grams) Epsom salt

1–2 cups (225–450 grams) sea salt (I would opt for salt from the Dead Sea for the bath and use other sea salts, such as salt from the Mediterranean or Himalayan, in the kitchen, but any salt you have on hand will work.)

Additional offerings:

Pinch of baking soda

Essential oils or fresh herbs that invigorate the senses, such as rose petals, lavender, or fresh rosemary

DIRECTIONS

After you soak in a hot bath with the salts for at least 10–15 minutes, wrap yourself in a towel and get under both the bed sheets and covers up to your chin while still wrapped in the towel. Sweat it all out of your pores before kicking off the covers and either showering to rinse off or wiping yourself down and going to sleep. Only do a detox bath before bed. It will make you very sleepy. Drink plenty of water during the whole process.

If you are doing a detox bath at the onset of a new season of weather or because you are not feeling well, then in addition to drinking plenty of water, feel free to take grapefruit juice (or any other juice of your choice) and dilute it with water and a pinch of sea salt for added hydration. Himalayan sea salt is best for this, but any sea salt that can be used for cooking can accomplish the goal.

The Main Course

"Be brave enough to find the life you want
and courageous enough to chase it."
—Madalyn Beck

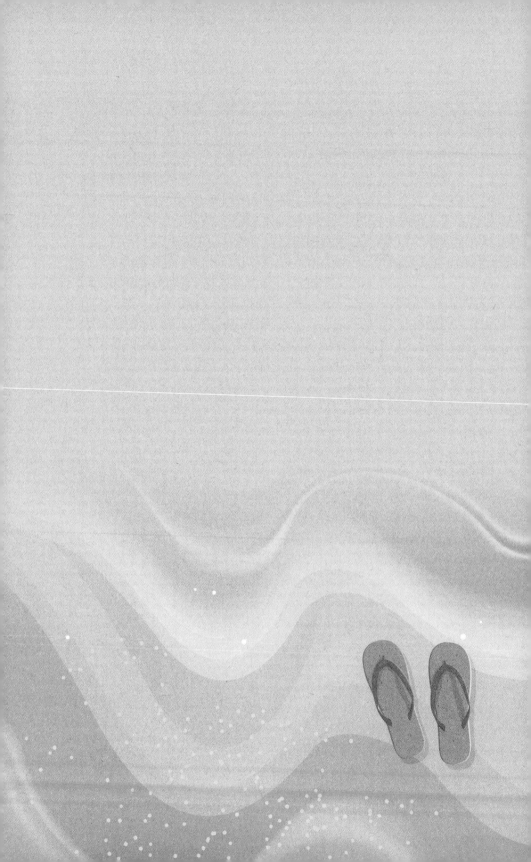

Chapter 5

It's About Community

I was speaking recently with one of my very best friends, Juliana, about what it is exactly that makes us so happy living here in Malta. She is from a Korean family and was born and raised in Brazil, and sometimes I forget that she is not American, as she lived in the US for a short time and carries a familiar American accent. She and her family are *my people*. She feels like home to me. My friendship with Juliana, her husband, and their children formed quickly and deeply. I consider them like family. We met because her son reached out to my incredibly shy child one day in class and told her, "If you ever feel left out or like you want to play but don't feel comfortable to ask to join, just come and get me and I will make sure that I bring you in."

From that day forward, once we met for a playdate at a local park, we were all hooked. We have celebrated every holiday, every birthday, Sunday Fundays, and daily park plays after school ever since. I love them with my whole heart and am so grateful that we found one another here. We are surely kindred spirits, she and I. We have very similar ways of appreciating our lives here in Malta. In fact, when we shared our Instagram handles, we discovered that they are the same three words in a different arrangement. You can't make this stuff up! We are both so incredibly grateful that this is our life now, and we work hard not to take for granted the blessings that have been bestowed upon us.

Juliana said something the other day when I was speaking about my life before versus now and how happy I am living here. She said, "That's because here it is a community. It is a different way of life than it was in America. Everything is so spread out and people are so independent there. But here, everything is close and centered around a community-based way of life."

I hadn't thought of it in quite those terms before, but she is exactly right. Where I come from, I had many friends who were seeking what is referred to as an "intentional community," those people who live slightly off the grid and live as a community. These communities are not easy to find and are populated with the best hippies you can imagine. I have always enjoyed visiting friends in any intentional community, but I never made one my home. Here in Malta, it is the natural way of life. You do not have to find land to build on together, because it's already built that way. You don't have to be invited and it's not a members-only sort of club. Here, you help your family, neighbors, friends, and even strangers. If you don't have family, people will help you find one that will take you in as their own. It is not something you have to seek out so much. It is everywhere here. You just have to make yourself available and be clear in your intention that this is the life you are looking for.

The first thing any local asks in Malta is how long you plan to stay, because that is how they will gauge whether to invest in the friendship or not. They often say that they need to know if we will be leaving after a short time because it breaks their hearts. Ever since I answered them with "we are here to make Malta our home," it has been no holds barred. Everyone has been so good to us. It is what this culture was founded on. I have never been around more generous, kind, caring, and passionate people. I feel like I'm truly at peace and at home and incredibly blessed to be included in it all.

I was riding in a cab the other day and the driver was local to Malta, born and raised. Whenever I'm in a cab here, I love to ask questions about where the person is from, what life was like for them if they came from another country, how they like Malta, etc. He told me that he lives in the Three Cities, which is a beautiful area just across from the capital of Valletta and known to be more of a locals-only area to live (meaning you grew up there and are fluent in Maltese). He said that the way he grew up there many years ago now, everyone would leave their house key still in the door so that anyone could walk in and check on them or visit them. He said that the residents of each house would make something to eat or drink and then they would sit outside and share all the meals to make it a celebration. This was not just for holidays, but daily! I feel like that is something you would see in movies but would never imagine was actually real. Stories like this are like chocolate to my soul.

Addiction or Liberation

You may currently feel very content with your life, and for that I am so glad. But there are many out there who feel quite unhappy or even displaced in their lives. Because I have been on both sides of that coin within a few years' range, I would like to take the time to discuss the value of community and connection and how they can deeply affect an entire life. Oftentimes, suffering people magnetize themselves to more suffering people, just the way that positive and happy people magnetize themselves to the more joyful ones. Misery loves company just as much as joy does. You may feel burned out, overworked, undervalued, or lost in trying to figure out what would make you truly happy as opposed to simply content, complacent, or, even worse, disconnected.

There is a common saying in addiction medicine that if the right crisis meets the right substance, anyone can become an addict. If those two things should intersect at just the right time, anyone can fall into the abyss of addiction. I would say that the things coming down the pipe with this pandemic alone could be enough to send anyone over the edge, not to mention the enormous and polarizing political divides happening all around the world. No one is immune to despair, no matter where they live.

Naturally, this got me pondering the idea that if anyone can fall into a world of addiction, what would be the antidote to that? If we are so unhappy with our lives that we have to rely on a behavior or substance to survive it from day to day, what would it look or feel like if we divorced ourselves from those habits and formulated a whole new way of living? And how would that process of formulating a whole new way of being actually play out?

There are many words that people have used to describe whatever they see as being the antidote to addiction. I've heard from recovering addicts that their description of the opposite word of addiction would be *freedom*. Many believe that the opposite of addiction is sobriety. While it stands to reason that sobriety would be the ideal candidate for the opposite of addiction, I don't entirely agree with that idea. There are a lot of sober people out there who fall in the category of being a "dry drunk," because they may be sober, but their behaviors never improved.

I've decided, for me at least, that the word that is the antidote to addiction is *liberation*. Liberation doesn't just leave you sober; it leads you to a higher level of operating without the constant attachment that the substance or behavior used to bring. The concept of liberation offers the advantage of living life from a place where you are no longer just in survival mode but instead are thriving.

To me, that is a much better ideal to strive for than simply getting clean or sober and free from any negative or dangerous patterns. You don't just break up with the behaviors; you move on to something that tastes better to your whole body and soul. No one is immune to destruction or addiction, so it stands to reason that no one is immune to reconstruction and liberation either!

The Rat Park Experiments

There is a man named Johann Hari who gave a TED Talk in which he famously announced that the opposite of addiction is not sobriety but rather human connection.[13] He went on to share a study done on rats to show the difference in what an increase or a decrease in basic interac-

13. Hari, "Johann Hari."

tions and connections can do. The study was part of the Rat Park, a series of studies conducted by a psychologist named Bruce Alexander and his colleagues and published between 1978 and 1981. Alexander studied single rats alone in cages and set out two kinds of water in each cage, one laced with drugs and the other pure drinking water. More times than not, the rats chose the water laced with drugs. They ultimately became addicted and died. Alexander concluded that the rats went for the water with the drugs because they were lonely and had no other stimulation.

Next he put rats together in new cages along with the same two types of water (one laced with drugs and the other pure drinking water) and then added food, toys, and tunnels, creating a funfest for them. He was testing to see if the rats from a different social situation would still choose the water with the drugs or would go for the clean drinking water. In his findings, some of the rats did drink both sets of water, but they never became drug-addicted and none of them died.

This same professor then went a step further and took already drug-addicted rats who were living alone in their cages and added them to the funfest cages with friends and toys to see if it would change which water they would choose. It turns out that the already drug-addicted rats who were placed in the cages with the others no longer went for the water that was laced with drugs![14]

The article that I pulled this information from, written by Michael Ascher, MD, referred to this study as an example of how human beings naturally crave human connection. We crave community. When these needs are not met, this is when we may likely turn to things like bad behaviors or substances to fill the void. Ascher was also trying to demonstrate that when our needs are being met and we can experience firsthand the bonding and loving actions of our fellow friends and neighbors, we can alter the patterns of our addictions and habits.

It is written into our genetic code to crave human connection and community. We know this. We have always known this. But we have let

14. Ascher, "The Opposite of Addiction Is Not Sobriety—It Is Human Connection."

those connections slip away all too easily and we must work hard to get them back. We need each other. We always have. We always will.

IRL (In Real Life)

We have to get back to in-person communication the best way we can. We need more hugs and hand-holding. Touch is something so magical and so vital to us all. As a hands-on bodyworker for almost twenty years, I know the effect that physical contact of a kind, loving, and professional nature can have on a person. I have witnessed many people break down and cry because they have not experienced being touched in such a long time. When I hug someone I love, I hug them tight, moving my face to one side and then the other, so that we can connect heart to heart, fully and completely. Never underestimate the power and importance of human touch. There is much research to be found on the benefits to our health and wholeness from a sincere hug.

Remember that while many of us have spent so much time building our brands on Instagram or Facebook, it's not real life. Social media can be a wonderful asset to any business, but your business is not your life. Sometimes we forget this and define ourselves by *what we do* rather than *who we are*. We need to connect with people and do so face-to-face as much as possible. Finding any sort of community can have a hugely positive impact on our lives. Never underestimate the power of feeling included. Let's enjoy a laugh, a smile, or a cry. Let's make time to get to know one another and relearn how to show up for each other in a deeper way. This nugget of wisdom has been a game-changer for me.

The real heroes of my life in the Mediterranean are my dear friends and loved ones who encourage me to get out and enjoy life more. Surrounding myself with people who want to be outside and get out and about has been such a deeply needed breath of fresh air. Even during a worldwide pandemic, I have been able to be more social and be outside more than I have in years! It doesn't hurt that we are surrounded by the sea. Everywhere you drive, you will find a view of the water. If you are a water person, you know exactly what I'm saying here. It's like your whole soul opens up and every breath changes with awareness and awe.

Life in the Mediterranean

I will be the first to admit that I had gotten incredibly lazy at maintaining friendships from afar through the tools of social media rather than in-person communication long before I could use Covid as an excuse. Then when it hit, learning to maintain friendships from afar became a necessity and not a chosen priority. The world closed down and relationships formed through new avenues. In many ways, this has been an amazing blessing both personally and professionally for quite a lot of people all around the world. Some people thrive doing things online much more than in person, while others desperately need to maintain relationships in person. While many people lost their jobs, other people were able to land their dream jobs working remotely.

There is a place for digital communications to be sure. But we can't risk getting entrenched in it to the point that we lose the ability to prioritize in-person relationships. Whether our situation allows only for online communications or we desire to live in a world offline, we can't deny that the persona we create online may not be the person we are in real life. Filters abound to change the way we look, the way we communicate, and the persona we may have created for ourselves and use as our front. It used to be an effort simply to work to achieve a balance of who we are on the inside with what we do and say on the outside. Now we have to contend with who we are in real life as opposed to what we feel on the inside, what we show on the outside, and what we put out into the digital cloud of everything we say and do. To live authentically comes with so many more layers to it than ever before. Who we are IRL is the garden in which everything we plant begins to grow.

The idea that you maintain relationships through anything technology-based here in Malta is unacceptable. The island is small and reminds me of my high school and college days, where you could jump in the car and be at anyone's place in ten minutes if someone wanted to see you or needed you. When I first arrived here and started making friends, I met my first friend, Michelle. As we were getting to know each other, she laid down the law with me: "If you want to be in my life, you have to put in the effort to be here. I will put in the effort, too. But I won't put in the effort if I'm the only one doing it."

Michelle reminded me that you have to show up for your friends! You have to make time to keep people in your life. Relationships of any kind cannot be one-sided if you expect them to be in balance. They have to mean enough for you to get yourself near them and enjoy your very valuable time together.

It is so much easier to get together when you live in a smaller area, and with the weather being as lovely as it is here most days, it's easy to get out more and join up with people. I did not do that in the US anywhere near as often as I do now. I don't think a week goes by where I don't have some sort of meetup with a friend or two here. I was a very well-established hermit where I lived before, and I thought I preferred it that way. It turns out I don't! All it takes is some sunshine, some water, and some really lively people to get me up and out. The trilogy lives! Sun, water, and people are my three to be!

The good thing is that even if you can't up and move to a tiny island out in the middle of the sea, this is where social media *can* help you! There are tons of expat groups on social media sites where people who live all over the world come together to check in on their friends local to the island areas. You can join all sorts of groups and see photos and hear the good and the bad of island living. We hear tons of gripes on our expat sites, which I try to avoid since I am still in the honeymoon phase of living on the island and have no desire to be directed anyplace else with my opinion. You can even begin by putting up large posters of the environments that you are considering for a change. Maybe put up images of the sea and sailboats and notice how it makes you feel to look at them, or of the snowcapped mountains or other places with different weather and surroundings and see if anything changes your perspective or opens your mind to new possibilities.

The happiness and gratitude for life are not unique to me. Every member of my family who moved here feels the same way. We are all noticeably happier and calmer people. There is a sense of peace within us that comes from being less distracted by so many outside stimuli. Being outside in nature reminds us that simple, natural, and real life is just beyond our doors, not on the open screen or tablet. We didn't put those things down; they just don't consume us the way they used to. We feel the need to walk after a large meal or go explore. Our basic sense of adventure has returned to us as if we were children. This doesn't mean we are out taking hikes or even taking sailing classes. It means that if we eat out anywhere, we walk around wherever we are before heading back home. Malta is an extremely populated country, so you are always out and about walking among many other people. It's like social walking after a meal. Just a little bit makes you feel better.

Sunday Fundays

The house that we rent is the perfect gathering place for parties, so we host what we call Sunday Fundays weekly in summer and less frequently during the colder months when the pool is not part of the equation. The different families we host hail from all around the world, and I love to soak in as much of their cultures as I possibly can. As soon as the families arrive, everyone pairs off into groups. The children immediately go to find one another, the women tend to gravitate to each other, and the men head straight outside. Each family brings a side dish to share. My husband always grills the meats, so you tend to find several men all hanging out near the grill sharing drinks and later in the day sharing cigars. By the pool, there are long tables and chairs for everyone to sit together and eat, followed by a second table for the children to sit together and enjoy their meals. Long tables are an absolute must outside and inside the homes here. In every home I have been to that has the space, long tables have a place.

I have learned so much listening to the different people from various countries offer their wisdom. Sometimes they remind you that the way you are preparing something is entirely wrong. Then they emphatically yet hilariously take over, and if you are like me, you take a step back and watch them with wonder as they get to work and take it all in. Sometimes I feel like I'm living in a scene from the movie *Under the Tuscan Sun*. Other times I feel like I'm part of *My Big Fat Greek Wedding*. So many of the things from those movies are true! I see it more and more as I spend time with my Greek friends especially. Since those are my two favorite movies, what I now call my home feels like a perfect mix of both, plus a pinch of *Game of Thrones* (season one was filmed here in Malta), all mixed together to create a new dish that tastes sweet, spicy, and genuinely crafted. I find these people to be so lively and hilarious. What a joy it is to get to be the host of such gatherings!

Family First

I believe that faith, family, and food are the three tenets of life here. Besides shared faith, family takes priority every single time and food is the glue that brings it all together. Luckily for us, once you become close friends, you also are taken in as part of the family. The depth of friendship and support here blows my mind. This is the kind of thing you see in the movies and don't realize that it is not for show. This is how the Mediterranean culture thrives: with family, with friends, with wine, olive oil, and a long dining table to serve the many courses of meals they share. The Maltese seem to be able to accommodate any time of day for a gathering and a meal, but dinner seems to be the large meal that they share with family and friends. This goes on for hours into the night, with local wine and fresh bread from the local baker along with the local cheese known as *ġbejna* on every table.

My Greek friends tell me that lunch is the largest meal for them, not dinner, even for celebrations. The Greeks on this island all seem to know one another. There are Greek groups where the families stick close and support each other. No matter who you meet, if they are Greek and you ask, "Hey, do you know this family?" the answer is always yes! You know how each state in the US is populated by millions and yet we always ask if you know the one person who lives in the state or area of anyone we meet and the answer is always some form of hilarious no? Well, in Malta, that is not the case. The answer seems to always be yes!

The Maltese are almost all related in some form or fashion or are only one to two degrees of separation from any name you drop. The Italians who live here don't seem to be as interconnected, but I think that's because Italy is so huge that things don't operate in the same manner. They say that Italy is basically like three distinct countries: southern Italy, northern Italy, and then the central part. Malta is only sixty miles from Sicily, so the Sicilians all seem to know each other over here. And the few people from Spain that I've met all seem to prefer their homeland to anyplace else in the world and tend to stick close to each other the most. Everyone I have met from any of the surrounding countries is extremely proud to be from that place. They take great pride in their heritage and their families. Malta is certainly no exception.

Everyone here in Malta knows each other. Once you meet new people, you start to see them out and about everywhere on the island. I have yet to meet people here from any of the surrounding Mediterranean countries who are not loud, proud, and incredibly fun-loving. They also all seem to have unspoken rules that everyone from their country is in perfect agreement on. I find it insightful and take in all that I can. I love learning their rules and beliefs. This applies to foods especially. The Maltese are known for their incredible bread. Their loaves of bread are subsidized by the government and therefore are sold at extremely low prices so that everyone can afford to eat good bread. A Maltese loaf of bread (looks like mountain bread) costs less than one euro. Every Greek I've met will be sure to let me know that their Greek bread is the best. The biggest competition seems to be over bread, wine, and olives especially. My French and Italian friends will of course say that they win in all three categories as well. The French especially win in the wine, cheese, bread, and cream departments. This makes the different party trays very enjoyable!

While I am advocating for in-person communications and being who you really are both online and in real life, I also understand that not everyone will get the opportunity that I did to change everything about their current situation and go live the kind of life that fairy tales are made of. There were many years when I followed people on social media who were living the life of my dreams, and I reacted in two ways: I was totally jealous and a little bit resentful and I also turned them into my blueprint for better living and what I wanted from my life.

Begin small by doing group chats, zoom meetings, and digital hang-outs. If you want to move locations, beef up your resume and begin to float it in places you may not have considered before. Use social media to start digging around in things you would like to see and do in your life. Save up and take a vacation to the destination you are seriously considering as your dream place and put yourself out there. That is your best bet to land a job there, if you are available for an interview in person while you are visiting. This is your life! Do not waste it wishing constantly to be someplace or someone else without doing some form of preparation in order to ask the universe to throw you a curveball toward something awesome.

Things Will Show Up When You Do

If you want to find your people, you have to show up at the place where you are hoping they will be. This is a recipe for soul-nourishing joy and a reminder that you have the power to add something more delicious to your life. Maybe you will meet your person. Maybe you will meet your new best friend. Maybe you won't make any new friends, but you might find something that brings a new purpose and joy to whatever you are doing. The payoff for being brave will be equal to the risk you are willing to take to construct something new in your life.

When you make a change in your life and commit to it, other amazing opportunities begin to line up and magnetize themselves to you. When you add something of significance to your life, you are guaranteed a new outcome. No new spice is added to a dish that goes undetected.

Every spice we throw in will have an instant effect on what we added it to. We don't necessarily get to choose what that full dish will be, but the new spice will alter the dish and transform it into something else. You are guaranteed to be offered a purpose in it.

As a person who struggled desperately in school, I still believe that there is nothing more valuable in the entire world than education. That does not limit my description of *education* to a traditional school as the only option. It could mean learning to garden or bake. The key word here is *learning*. When you take it upon yourself to increase your knowledge of any specific concept, you increase your education on the subject. Reading more books about something that fascinates you will expand your knowledge base. Knowledge is power. Education offers a pathway deeper into that power. Sign up for a photography class, a dance class, or anything that will allow you to learn even basic information and convert it into a personal sense of wellbeing and power.

Food for Thought: Your Current Community

Community is such a big subject to think about. When it comes to creating the community that supports who you are today and who you might morph into tomorrow, those people can be very challenging to find. No matter where you live, there are people everywhere who are of like mind with the person you are in this moment. They are always out there and willing to accept you into their group, which leads to bigger questions:

- Is the community that would match who you are right now in this moment one you really want to be a part of? Why?
- Where are you now and who do you want to be? How well do the two match up?

I have mentioned this before in other books of mine because the following three questions remain the most important questions that I ask myself almost every single day. If I follow the guidance of these three questions, it never leads me astray. These answers keep me balanced and focused and moving in a direction toward something greater.

1. Who are you? In this moment, today, who are you? What are you about? What do you stand for? This is a much deeper question than a simple answer can express. It is the foundation on which everything else is built. Who are you in the most honest and vulnerable way?

2. What do you want? This is not about cars or money. I mean what do you really want out of life? What do you really want for yourself with the time you have remaining on this planet?

3. Here is the biggest game-changer question of all: What are you willing to do to get it? This separates daydreams from dreams realized. How far are you willing to put yourself out there in order to make question number 2 come to life?

Food Tip and Recipe

There is a bread here known as *ftira* that makes up the majority of the Maltese sandwiches. Ftira is a round, flattened sourdough bread. Sandwiches made with the Maltese ftira are served in all the cafés no matter the time of year or even the time of day. They can be a lunch, a breakfast, or a dinner. They are served at gatherings and in lots of different ways. In 2020 the Maltese ftira was the first local product to be added to UNESCO's Intangible Cultural Heritage of Humanity List. On the official site, it is quoted that ftira "fosters a shared identity in Malta, bringing people together in homes and workplaces."[15] The announcement also adds that it requires a skilled baker to be able to make this incredible bread by hand.

Interestingly, much of the local bread is made by prisoners by hand daily for the residents. The Corradino Correctional Facility is home to the oldest oven on the island. On the week of Good Friday, they sell their bread to the public and donate the proceeds to charity. It is estimated

---

15. Magri, "Maltese Ftira Added to UNESCO's Intangible Cultural Heritage List."

that in 2013, over 2,000 Maltese loaves of bread, nearly 4,000 buns, and over 1,000 French sliced loaves were produced at the prison weekly.[16]

I was fortunate enough to visit the prison bakery after doing this research. I was able to do an interview for my column on the residents who make the bread. The residents who work in the bakery were incredibly kind and generous in sharing their bread with us and how it gets made. We arrived at 6:00 a.m. to see it all happening in real time. You cannot imagine the synchronicity that is involved when the dough reaches the table. It's a long table and several men stand on either side of it. The man at the top, who I'll call the chopper, first measures the handheld blade to be sure it's at 150 grams and then begins to cut into the dough and separate and pass it down in a manner that sounds like a drumbeat or a bass chord.

Then it becomes a full-on symphony of sounds: *chop, chop, chop* sounding exactly like *1, 2, 3* and then the swipe of the dough sliding over the flour and into the hands of anyone who grabs it first. From there, the men quickly put their hands around it and form a perfect circle, no matter if the piece of dough is large or small for buns or for loaves. Then they pass it down to the end of the table, where the men there put it in a large box lined with parchment paper and properly floured and then take it to the fire oven. The sounds of the *chop, swirl,* and *swoosh* are meditative. I got lost in them. This bakery is a tight-knit community of residents who work there just doing the best they can with a newfound set of skills and a work ethic that will help to support them when they are in the outside world again.

The oven heats to 550 degrees Celsius (1022 Fahrenheit). They place the loaves along a large wooden shovel-like tool called a *peel*. It has a long wooden lever with a large, flat surface at the top. The oven is a wood-fired oven and is enormous beyond description. That's why they can place so many loves beyond the head of the peel and along the wooden handle to get them all to easily fill in the space of the oven. They put in around six

---

16. Times of Malta, "Sneaking a Peak behind the Prison Walls."

loaves at a time for one single row and then make several rows across to bake.

In Malta, in the colder months especially, soups make up at least one daily meal, along with fresh bread. The bread here does not have preservatives in it like we are used to in the US, and therefore we need to buy bread fresh daily or every other day. It stays good for only two days before it starts to mold. I know people here who have their bread delivered to them daily by the local bakers. Not much here is mass-produced, and the locals pride themselves on that fact. The bread makers still do it all by hand. The jam makers still do it kilo by kilo.

As I mentioned, a Maltese ftira sandwich is one of the most common foods offered in homes and at local cafés and bakeries alike. If you are a local, you won't refer to it as a ftira, you will call it a Ħobż biż-żejt. I was introduced to it simply as a ftira. These are round, flattened sourdough bread sandwiches usually with fillings of tuna, potatoes, capers, eggs, kunserva (tomato paste), olive oil, and other vegetables. These sandwiches are served all over the island.

If you do not live in the Mediterranean countries where ftira bread can be easily found, look for a circle loaf of bread at any bakery or deli, or you can always use a fresh ciabatta or something similar. Also, the kunserva that this recipe calls for is a tomato paste that is local to Malta, which you can also find in Australia, as they are shipped there from Malta. You can use a tomato paste substitute (preferably not ketchup) or just skip it (though with kunserva, it tastes remarkably better). Once you have your fresh bread, cut it in half, spread the tomato paste on the bottom side, and then drizzle it with olive oil (or you can wait and drizzle the olive oil on top of everything). Then add a sprinkling of ingredients listed here to your preference.

The Maltese Ftira (Ħobż biż-Żejt)
(Recipe by Michelle Abela)

The translation of Ħobż biż-żejt to English is "bread with oil." What follows is a long list of ingredients, but everything is optional according to preference. People often make a Ħobż biż-żejt with sliced hard-boiled eggs and other vegetables or add potatoes or butter beans to either the egg version or the tuna version. There is no limit to what you can add, but always finish with a generous drizzle of olive oil.

INGREDIENTS

Ftira bread (or round, flat sourdough bread), sliced in half horizontally

Kunserva (or tomato paste), spread on the bottom half of the bread

Then layer any of the following options:

Anchovies or tuna

Green olives

Capers

Sundried tomatoes

Ġbejniet, Maltese peppered cheeselet, or peppered feta

Dried oregano, mint, and/or parsley

Cannellini beans or butter beans

Red onion

Cucumber slices

Fresh mint, chopped finely, or dried mint, used sparingly

A small sprinkle of salt and pepper

Top with a generous drizzle of fine extra virgin olive oil.

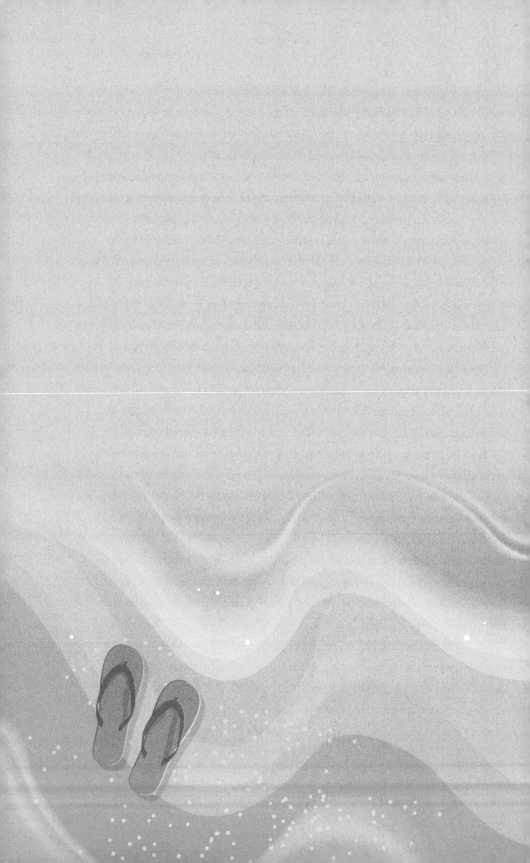

Chapter 6

Time and Thyme Again

This chapter will cover the value of timing and not missing your chances when opportunities come at a particular time. Timing is everything, and we need to learn patience and respect for the process as it unfolds. We must be willing to take advantage of opportunities and work with them when they appear. When opportunity knocks, we had best run to the door.

Timing Is Everything

I remember when I was much younger, a person said that when it comes to relationships, 10 percent is attraction and 90 percent is timing. At the time, that didn't make a lot of sense to me. I would have switched those numbers around. As I have grown older and observed just how import-ant timing is to things, I see that this might have been a very sage offering of wisdom. Timing is crucial to manifesting anything new. How many times in our lives have we met someone or attempted to do something but the timing was just not right? There is a specific time and place for opportunities to be built or squashed. Companies all over the world have invented products that were ahead of their time and so they failed, only to find the same thing come out a few years later and hit pay dirt. It's in the timing.

Some people are ahead of their time, while others are frantically try-ing to catch up to the current times. The hardest part of this concept is trusting it. Trusting is not a passive response. You must be fully involved in the process and fully aware of the timing that is unfolding around you. You step into that flow and work with the timing. If it's a bust, know when to step out and walk away. None of this happens *to* you. None of this even happens *for* you. It happens *with* you.

I believe there are two types of timing: standard timing and divine timing. Standard timing can mean an array of different things. Showing up on time is a timing thing. Waiting for your turn in line is a matter of timing, as is doing your daily routines, like getting up on time, going to bed on time, setting an alarm, etc. Divine timing, however, is more like the answer to one of life's riddles, like being late to something only to find out you just missed a major accident, or going back into the store because you forgot something only to meet your future life mate in the pet food aisle. Everything that happens has some sort of magic behind it that is bigger than you. There is a force behind our opportunities and decisions and the time it takes to make them real. The intersection of timing and purpose creates an entirely new path. Timing + purpose = the pathway to greatness. That is my mathematical equation of what happens when divine timing leads the way and we don't resist.

As an example, we were proposing the move to Malta a year earlier, but it did not work out. That is a timing thing. It wasn't the right time. Instead, we moved someplace else. It was a place that kept my soul in a stale state instead of nourishing it, but it was an important step nonetheless. The timing was not yet right for our massive breakthrough into our dream life. When the timing was right and all the stars aligned, we were able to make this move, even amid complete and utter worldwide chaos as the whole world locked down. Why? Divine timing was at play here. This was a *meant to be* deal for us. There is no doubt in my mind that this move was divinely guided. I could feel it in my bones.

The Caveat

Just because our move to Malta was divinely guided and timed perfectly does not mean it was easy. Notice that I describe life here as being *sim-*

pler as opposed to *easier*, because divine timing does not offer any kind of free access. It simply offers the opportunity and a path at exactly the right time to come to life should you choose to take it. You still have to choose to jump and you will still face plenty of hurdles.

Getting here was excruciating. Every test was thrown down for us to pass in order to cross the divide. Our passports were lost and locked in boxes, and because of the pandemic, the passport offices closed for months. I had to get a local politician to intervene and get my renewed passport out of the vault from a different state than the one where my children's passports had been issued, even though they had all been processed at the same time in the same location. Getting our pets here was a nightmare and required me to be relentless and bold in making it happen.

There was not a day for months when I was not on the phone constantly pushing to find someone nice enough to help me with the various items on my list that had to be completed. We were the last people allowed into this country before they closed their borders to everyone. We got our papers during our layover in the Netherlands. Talk about trusting the process! Holy moly, it was not easy! But the opportunity was available and we did not balk along the way. We set our sights on our goal and fixed ourselves to it as we made our way halfway around the world with children and pets to a place we had never once even visited. I realize now that not only was divine timing at play but so was absolute blind faith. We had to trust every single move along the way to get us here. Then we had to close our eyes and jump.

Divine timing creates an opportunity, but you must do the rest. If you want to change your life, it probably won't look nearly as dreamy as your imagination might have you believe, but you have to trust the possibility that there is something so much greater for you out there if you trust it and go for it. Timing sets up the parameters, but it's up to you to do the rest. If you are looking for a change in any aspect of your life that asks you to be brave, you cannot afford to waver. You have to be smart and establish all your possibilities and then make a heartfelt leap directly into the center.

Divine timing is a key foundation for manifesting. It is the opportunity to jump into a new aspect of life. It paves a path for you to walk through. It does not necessarily make things *easy*; it just makes things *possible*. I believe that we are here for a reason and that I have not even scratched the surface of how deeply those reasons are rooted. I trust this process more than I have ever trusted any big change in my life. I feel supported spiritually, financially, physically, and emotionally. I have made plenty of moves in my life where I felt none of those things. Timing is one thing, but divine timing is something elevated that provides a link to a place of supreme and utter bliss. The Mediterranean to me is Heaven on Earth. I spent a great deal of time learning to respect the guidelines of divine timing and how to trust that process. I've seen it line up and come to life too many times to doubt the magic behind the manifest.

The Garage Made Me Do It

I moved into a dream-life scenario coming here. We chose a home through a local realtor who sent us email after email of homes for rent. We had no clue about the location of any of them. We had no idea what life we would be choosing based on which home was available. It came down to two final choices, and our realtor then made appointments to go to each home and take multiple videos for us to be able to make the most informed decision. Every time I would ask her for her advice, she would be careful not to sway our decision with her own personal opinion. Then we closed our eyes, jumped into the deep end of the pool, and chose a new home from a million miles away.

The deciding factor was the garage. One option had a garage that was detached and across the street from the house, but the location was in the heart of a lovely town that we have since grown to adore. Our life would look completely different had we chosen that place. We were so close to signing that lease until the moment I saw that garage on the realtor's video, which conjured images of me holding two little children's hands while carrying groceries and trying to cross the street. Two days after seeing that video, we ended up in a bidding war for the house we have now. We won. It was always meant to be ours. Now I know with certainty that it was never meant to be any other way than exactly how it played out.

It turns out that the home we chose was divinely guided to absolute perfection within the confines of what *perfect* could be. We moved into a home that was built by a set of parents for their three children. The three children are now grown and rent the home in order not to cause tension between them by having to choose which one would live there. Not only this, but the person we rent from, the main woman we work with, Doreen, has become one of my very best friends. She feels like family to me. She also lent me her own best friend, Michelle, and together the three of us have carved out a new and very valuable relationship with one another. We are the body, mind, and soul of something new and beautiful between ourselves. They are two of the best friends a person could ever wish for in the world. They show up for me in ways I had no idea was possible. That's not because I don't have amazing friends back home, but life before looked completely different from life here. Michelle, Doreen, and I make a date with each other every weekend. We try never to miss our date time together. It is a time that I treasure to share a coffee and a chat with them. Our families all know that sometime over the weekend they will need to fend for themselves, because the three of us are going out on a date with each other by ourselves.

Living someplace small allows everyone to live mere minutes away from each other, no matter where you live on the island. Doreen started accepting our invitations to bring her family to our Sunday Fundays by the pool in summer after weeks of me asking her to come. This year we were finally able to bring my mom over for her first visit. As a gift, I had some friends play the piano for her. It was like Chopin, Beethoven, and Bach all came over for a visit that day. Each song was played brilliantly, and the room (even full of children) stayed silent as we all watched in awe at the magnificence of each of the musicians. Music is a huge part of the culture here in Europe. Many people have spent a lifetime learning to play their instruments. My mother's father was a lifelong musician. He raised ten children on a career in music, playing in the symphony and in jazz clubs by night. I brought everyone in from the pool and told my mother I had a gift for her. At first she was embarrassed, until she realized it was the gift of music. She thought it was the greatest thing when our friends played the piano for her.

To me, the best part of all was the moment I looked over to find Doreen standing still with giant crocodile tears streaming down her face as she watched. She was frozen solid in extreme emotion, all-consuming love. Afterward she said to me, "This is the greatest summer of my life. This is everything I have prayed for with this house. This is the best gift." That meant the world to me to be able to give her even a smidgen of what life here has given us. This year, our second Christmas in Malta, she had us join her whole family for the festivities. This family is all heart. This is what truly generous and loving people do here. You are friends first who become family.

If we had moved the year before like we had planned, the house we live in now would not have been an option. It was not on the market then. It was occupied by a different family leading a different life, one that did not invite the owner over for Sunday Fundays. We would have had to choose from a different set of homes to rent, and I never would have met my very best friends. If that is not divine timing meets opportunity, I do not know what is. To think, even for a moment, that my life would have unfolded any differently than exactly how it has here, I can't even entertain the thought.

An Opportunity Is Yours for the Taking

If you are reading this and wishing for a different life or a better way, I want to validate that there can be a path created somewhere that allows it to be so, but it might not be granted to you immediately just because you asked for it. Just know that once you do ask for a new path, one will begin being created for you, but you must be willing to play. It's a process that you have to be fully invested in and stick with as it unfolds. I have always believed that once you make your mind up, the universe will do something to test your resolve. It wants to gauge your level of commitment by offering you something very tempting to make you stay. It's the equivalent of when you finally get away from your last breakup and start to see someone else, and the last breakup shows back up simply to test your level of commitment to staying broken up and starting something new.

It's always easier to remain in any given circumstance. We are creatures of habit by nature. Staying in what we know is the typical approach to life. Letting go and creating something new requires not just bravery but also a willingness to get messy and to be open to changes that might be earthquakes to your very core. Even though our life here has turned out to be incredible, I could just as easily point out the flaws. There are some hard parts to be sure. Here in Malta specifically, the flaws do not compare to the gains, so I choose not to fixate on them. It's not even a contest. All of it was worth it.

If you are putting something in motion and are committed to that shift, trust the timing and the path to get there. Do not give up on what has the strongest pull on your soul. If something from deep within continues to whisper its calling to you, never push that voice away. Ask for help to make it happen. Trusting the timing will surely test your resolve, but just remind yourself that timing dictates the outcome—every single frustrating time.

The Prisoner and the Bird

When I got to visit the Corradino Correctional Facility to interview the men who worked in the bakery, there was something I noticed that felt very poignant. There was a single bird that kept flying into the bakery and back out. It would fly in and perch from up high and watch for a few moments and then fly back out into the sunshine again to the nearest tree branch. Then it would fly back into the bakery again. It was like he lived there: the resident bird—the only thing in there that was not actually caged. It made me think of Maya Angelou's book *I Know Why the Caged Bird Sings.* I pointed him out and one of the residents said he usually comes with two other birds. Especially in winter, they wait to get inside. He said the three birds do this all day, flying in and out that way. I also realized the obvious: the bird was there for the bread crumbs. He might be the smartest bird in all of Malta. He knows just where to go to get the good stuff! And when the residents were putting the loaves of bread through the slicing machine just before bagging them, the bird stood peacefully on the ground beneath the machine and ate the crumbs. No one bothered the other. It was all good.

There are so many birds on the island who are locked in tiny cages and set outside people's houses as a living decoration. It makes me very sad when I see them in the smallest cages and I wonder what pleasure anyone gets from keeping them held so tightly, so deeply against their very nature, and somehow they feel no guilt for doing it to them. Now I'm standing in a prison and everything is the other way around. The birds are the only ones who can come and go as they please and the people are the ones locked in the cage.

We often talk about the birds who never realize when their cage door is open so that they are free to fly out. In this case, with the inmates, they are unable to go free anywhere but within the confines of the community they keep. Quite a few were quick to tell me how long they have served and how much time they have left. Time means something completely different to these residents. I can't put it into the category of divine time or even basic time. This measure of time is tied completely to both restriction and freedom. The concept of time in this place is something beyond definition. But the bird that day…that bird was the one to fly free, and I felt it.

It's About Thyme

Thyme is an herb that is indigenous to the Mediterranean. The derivation of the word *thyme* has two meanings. One is to fumigate and the other is an herb to infuse food with. With its intense aroma, thyme has been used in burial ceremonies dating back as far as embalming rituals can be traced. Thyme has been used in many ceremonies to bury and honor the dead and to ward off or rid oneself of the darkness. My friend's grandmother in Malta used to take leaves of thyme and leaves from an olive tree and mix them with salt and add a bit of olive oil to a cooking pan, and then waft the smoke and the fumes around the house to ward off bad spirits. Thyme is steeped in Greek and Roman mythology. It symbolizes strength and power, courage and sacrifice. The thyme sprig was embroidered on the togas of the generals and offered to knights before they went into battle to offer them strength.[17]

The herb thyme is a fragrant plant that is known for its woody notes and lavender blooms and grows naturally and wildly in Malta and all along the Mediterranean. It is used as a potent layer in flavoring both sweet and savory dishes, as the longer the thyme is cooked, the more flavor your dish will get from it. Thyme is often paired with other herbs, such as marjoram, rosemary, and sage. It is used to enhance flavor and reduce the gaminess of meats such as lamb and rabbit. It is also widely used in soups. In Spain, thyme is used in the preparation of olives. If you are aiming for a savory dish, thyme is usually a welcome guest at that party. Thyme is also used in certain desserts. It is one of the most versatile and heavily used herbs in these areas.

Thyme grows all over the Mediterranean and is indigenous to Malta. In Malta, wild thyme is protected, and it is against the law to harvest it. This precious herb is not just an asset to cooking savory dishes but is also vital to the production of honey. I spoke with a local Gozitan beekeeper by the name of Joseph about the wild thyme flowers and what they mean to the honeybee. He said, "Thyme flowers flourish from the start of May through the end of May only. It blooms not more than three weeks." The bees make honey almost all year long in order to feed themselves during the winter months, when they don't produce honey. However, we take that honey from them and they are left without. During these months,

17. National Records of Scotland, "Hairy Thyme."

the beekeepers feed them sugar syrup to nourish and keep them healthy until the spring season comes and wildflowers bloom again.

For bees and honey, the blooms from wild thyme bushes are among the most important and valuable flowers around. They are a beautiful lavender color and they spread across the islands just as the other wildflowers are dying and the remaining scenery is quickly changing from green to brown. The amount of rainfall we receive in the winter dictates how many flowers will bloom and for how long throughout the spring and summer months. All kinds of wildflowers bloom in the spring for the bees to forage. Then when those flowers are done, this is when thyme becomes the honeybee's hero.

Though the thyme bush blooms for no more than three weeks, this is the flower that keeps the bees in business. During those three weeks when the thyme bush is blooming, there aren't any other flowers in season. Clover is in season from March through May but is not often found in most areas and bees don't fly more than a two-mile radius from their hives. The bees will all rush to the thyme flowers and swallow the nectar whole. If you walk up to any thyme bush while it's in season, you will find that it will be full of bees. Joseph also says: "Thyme produces very rich honey. Though you can't tell what the honey was made from by its smell, you can tell which flowers by its color. Honey from thyme and clover offers a rich brown-colored honey, whereas honey from citrus blooms such as lemon and oranges is more yellowish. Honey from carob and eucalyptus trees is the darkest-colored brown honey."

I asked him about which flowers bloom during which months for the bees, and this is what he said: "Once thyme is done, it's prickly pear season. In June, the prickly pears bloom and the bees go to their flowers in the early morning. You can find six bees inside a single prickly pear flower." The blooms growing on the cactus that will become the prickly pear fruit are home to dancing bees that dive down to the bottom of the flowers and shimmy their way back up to pollinate. I could seriously watch the bees dance and shimmy in those yellow flowers on the cactus for hours. You can see them diving their way down into the flowers and dancing around the bottom until they look up and shake and shimmy their way back up and out. The prickly pears themselves do not show up until early August, at the hottest and driest time of the year—long after the bees have come and gone from the plant. Because the prickly pear grows everywhere here, it is easy to find a spot to watch the bees play in those flowers. I happen to have a prickly pear cactus overlooking my yard, and I often find myself taking a seat just to watch the joyful dance expressions of the bees. I find the dance of the honeybees to be an exceptional sight to see.

Joseph continued to say:

Also, in late June the caper flowers grow and the bees like to visit them late in the evening after 4:00 p.m. You will find that the caper blooms produce blue pollen. Then from mid-August to late August, the eucalyptus trees start blooming into mid to late September, followed by the carob trees in September and October. Then winter approaches and the bees do not produce honey during those months as the temperatures fall. This is when the bees are supposed to consume the honey that they made for themselves during spring and summer. In late January to the beginning of February, when the temperatures begin to come up a bit, the bees will start producing honey from the flowers and the beekeepers no longer need to feed them the sugar syrup.

The Waggle Dance

When a bee finds flowers to pollinate, it goes back to its hive and does something called the waggle dance. Located close to the entrance of the hive is an actual dance floor! This is where a honeybee will go and dance a jig to convey to the worker bees where the flowers are located. This waggle dance that bees do is incredibly intricate and fascinating. The bee that is sharing the information about the nectar through the waggle dance will indicate which direction the flowers are located by the angle of its own waggle. This tells where the nectar is in relation to the direction of the sun. The bee won't even be finished with its dance before the crew flies out to maximize the potential of getting to that nectar.

We could learn so much from the way the bees work together. Dancing, singing, wiggling, and waggling as part of their survival seems pretty cool to me! Even the bees teach us that life is meant to have a little bit more rhythm and rhyme to it, a little more shake and a lot more spice.

Timing, Thyme, and a Garden to Grow Figs

Timing really is everything. Divine timing and basic timing play such a huge part in how anything turns out in the end. It requires a very specific approach to when we plant the seeds in order to receive a bountiful harvest of everything we do in the world. This applies to growing food and it applies to our own soul purpose being in alignment with the universe. Whether or not we are lined up and in balance with the natural world and at the same time in balance with our spiritual energy can be seen and felt in lots of different ways. There is a sacred fruit among the islands and available in almost every country around the world that many believe was planted as an indicator of where your land is in relation to the Divine. When the people and the land are in alignment with all that is, the trees will yield a bountiful harvest. When the people or the land are at odds with anything around them, the trees will yield very little. This is the sacred fig tree.

There is much wisdom in the sacred spirituality of the fig. The Buddha first approached a mango tree on his hunt for the perfect place to sit and meditate. Instead, he chose a tree known scientifically as the *Ficus religiosa*, or a species of fig tree that he later named the Bodhi tree. He meditated under the tree for forty-nine days and reached enlightenment. In scripture, there are only two trees that are listed before the fig tree as a ceremonially spiritual gift of trees from God. It is said that God gives good gifts. When he gave Israel to the Jewish people, it was not just any old piece of land. God says in Deuteronomy 8:7–8, "The Lord your God is bringing you into a good land—…a land with wheat and barley, vines and fig trees, pomegranates, olive oil and honey."[18] There are seven types of food mentioned here, which would be abundant in the land promised to his people, and it is in the time leading up to the Jewish holidays when many of them are ripe and ready to be eaten. There is so much richness in what God has created and placed in this land for his people—not just in their good taste and nutrition but in their meaning too. And the fig is a fruit that crops up again and again in the scriptures because God does nothing without purpose. Many believe that it was never apples from the Garden of Eden that Eve ate, but instead figs. Adam and Eve used fig leaves to cover themselves as well.

Generally speaking, fig trees take a long time to cultivate and will require a farmer to tend to the crop for years to come. In biblical times, it is believed that fig trees were seen as a barometer of the state of health of the nation, "taken away as punishment and flourishing in times of restoration."[19] The hundreds of different varieties of fig trees all relay similar spiritual messages of abundance and prosperity. The fig is a fruit often associated with fertility and good health.

The fig is a fruit that is known as a symbol of both prosperity and a good life. It has been noted that "figs, like olives, are the quintessential Mediterranean fruit and one of the earliest fruits to be cultivated by man."[20] Figs are a treasure of these islands, and as the seasons go and different foods for different holidays come up, the figs while in season are a huge part of those dishes as both appetizers and desserts primarily. Figs are considered part of the savory section of a flavor profile, and once you taste them and explore the various varieties, it's easy to see why that is.

The Fig and the Wasp

I want to offer a bit about figs following the pollinating season of bees, because figs are not pollinated by bees. They are pollinated by the one and only fig wasp. Created specifically for fig trees, fig wasps only pollinate fig

18. One for Israel, "The Symbolism of Figs in the Bible."
19. Grapes and Figs Ministry, "The Fig Tree: What the Bible Says about Figs."
20. Jackson, "A Basket of Figs."

trees, and the figs can only be pollinated by fig wasps. It is a uniquely inter-dependent relationship. I think of it in a more spiritual context, as they were created exactly for each other. It's the perfect example of a symbiotic relationship. The need for the other is equally vital on both sides. Figs are such a succulent fruit and come in so many different varieties, and the only thing that can make them duplicate is a particular insect whose sole pur-pose in life is to be the link to their vitality. Neither can thrive without the other.

To get even more detailed about the wonders of nature and the fas-cinating treasures they hold, there are both male and female types of fig trees. The female fig tree pollinates first and the male trees follow at a later time. Here is where things get tricky—and tragic. The blossoms of the fig are found inside the fruit and do not have flowering branches (which is why bees are not pollinating them and unable to extract any nectar). The female fig trees, which blossom first, have the tiniest hole inside the blossom for the fig wasp to get inside and lay its eggs. The opening in which it must get through in order to land and nest is so tiny that the mama fig wasp will lose both her wings and her antennae trying to make her way into the area where she needs to go into in order to lay her eggs. She will then die there and be absorbed by a special built-in enzyme of the fig blossom.

Many believe that the body of the fig wasp is what gives fig meat that unique inside crunch, but it is not the reason for that added texture. The mama fig wasp basically gets swallowed up and becomes part of the fig tree itself. The eggs will then hatch and be small enough to easily get out of that hole and go to the next trees in order to pollinate. By contrast, when a fig wasp goes to a male fig tree to lay her eggs, the hole is wide enough that she will be able to release her eggs and fly back out.[21]

From there, whether it's a male or a female fig tree, the farmers become vigilant as they watch early morning every single day waiting to see the insects fly out from the trees and move to the other trees. This is

21. Wheeler, "The Unique Relationship Between the Fig and the Fig Wasp."

how they will know whether the tree will yield figs. Here in Malta, there are two seasons a year for the figs, depending on the different types of the trees. Once the first round of growth happens and clears, a second season will begin. In this way, figs are grown throughout many months of spring into summer and are used in various dishes accordingly.

There are many stories in the Bible that indicate that God planted figs throughout the different lands as a way of letting the people know by their yield of crop whether or not they were in good standing. During different earth cycles, the figs flourish, while at other times, the figs are showing us the dangers and destruction that are occurring. Many farmers cross-pollinate and basically create hybrids of different varieties of fig trees in order to create the sweetest and most resilient figs. The fig trees have a hard time in the hot, dry season, so the figs themselves have become a precious commodity on the islands. There has also been increased devastation due to the bark beetle that is eating away at our precious fig trees. Figs now cost almost double what they once did when the trees were producing more efficiently, and the availability of fresh figs is reduced. I consider the fig trees to be a barometer of the divisiveness of our people. It would be wise to pay attention and act with more kindness than we have been. It's time to be more aware of what nature is telling us.

Food for Thought: How Many Boats Did We Miss?

Everyone has a story they tell themselves that revolves around missing out on an opportunity that could have been really huge if they would have taken the chance and gone for it. This has everything to do with both basic and divine timing lining up in our favor. No one lives a life with zero regrets. But how important were those opportunities that we missed, anyway? Wasn't there a reason at the time that we didn't take a leap of faith? Was it lack of preparation? Lack of bravery? Lack of trust? Lack of faith? What was it, do you think, that made you step back and hope for another opportunity that felt more like your own?

I remember a client telling a story many years ago about how they believed that a visiting faith healer at their church was destined to heal a lifelong health condition they were dealing with. They believed with all their heart that if they would have had the courage to stand up that day and ask to be healed that they would have been. To them, it was the only option that was ever available to them to recover and it will never again come around. They missed it. They chickened out and so they will forever pay the price. They cling tight to that memory of solid regret and beat themselves up for not being brave enough to speak out when they had the chance. To this person, it means that they will never get that opportunity again.

This makes me sad because this person missed the most obvious part of the story. It proves that there is a part of them that truly believes there is an option to heal! Unfortunately, they won't allow themselves to believe that this particular healing is available to them. If you are not in line with the opportunity to heal, I can promise you that it will be next to impossible to recover fully. But once you open up to the idea that healing is possible, that is when everything can change.

Here are my questions for you:

- Can you think of a defining time in your life when you were given an opportunity to do something bold and brave but you didn't take it?
- How has that affected your life since that day?
- Did it change you?
- Did it make you shy away from ever trying it again?
- Do you believe that you only get one chance, and if you don't take that one that there will never be another chance again?

I want you to give a great deal of thought to this concept, and I want you to change the way you think about it with this added twist: if that boat that pulled up to port for you did not end up with you on it, do not doubt that another boat will come your way and right up to wherever you are docked. That is exactly the difference between standard timing and divine timing. Divine timing will not leave without you on that boat!

Divine timing has been waiting while you missed certain other opportunities to better prepare yourself for a bigger one to arrive for you. Divine timing carries with it the same shared energy as your divine creator. They never left you out!

Sometimes we miss opportunities because we simply were not ready to take them. But they were still necessary for our growth. The big opportunities that we think we missed are the ones that kept us going and working harder so that when the bigger boat started heading our way, we would recognize the flags and know that this one was ours and we would be ready. It will require your faith to trust that you will know it when you see it. That next big opportunity and outcome will be different too. It won't be the exact same thing you wanted before.

You are a different person now, and so is the boat that is coming to take you there. Different is not bad. Different is simply different. It will be something else that gets offered. It might be something better or it might be something comparable, but trust that it won't be something worse. As Glennon Doyle says in her book *Carry On, Warrior*, "You can't miss your boat. It's yours. It stays docked till you're ready. The only boat you can miss is someone else's. Let them have theirs while you wait for yours."

Who is to say that my client's visiting faith healer was there to heal them at all? When we think we missed an opportunity, maybe it wasn't actually our opportunity to miss! Maybe that opportunity was for the person beside us and was never ours! If you rethink those regrets and then put yourself in line for your own next big opportunity and commit yourself and prepare yourself to take it, what would stop this boat from being the one you've been waiting for all along? Those missed opportunities were just excuses for you to daydream about what could have been. Put that energy into what's ahead and prepare yourself for the moment when that boat shows up to take you there. Those things were never meant to be yours in the first place. You have to trust the timing. Ask yourself:

- What is meant to be yours now?
- What opportunities are you preparing for?

- Are you doing the work necessary to be able to take the opportunity when it shows up?
- Are you brave enough, strong enough, and trusting enough to board the bigger boat?
- Do you believe that divine timing will be on your side this time?

Food Tip and Recipe

Figs are the fruit of choice in Malta as soon as they are in season. We use them for many specialty and holiday dishes. A very simple recipe that can pair with any appetizer or main course theme is baked figs with goat cheese. It's very easy to prepare and will delight those at any dining table.

Baked Figs with Goat Cheese
(Recipe by Ariel Guivisdalsky)

This is a very simple way to bake figs. You can serve them either on a salad, if you want something sweet, or as a stand-alone appetizer.

INGREDIENTS

7 tablespoons (100 ml) port wine
Figs (1 per person)
Goat cheese that is not too salty
Thyme leaves
Sugar
Sea salt

METHOD

Reduce the port wine in a pan over heat until it is a thick glaze.

Cut the head of each fig crosswise and press the belly of it to open the top part slightly. Place some goat cheese and thyme leaves inside the open fig and sprinkle with sugar.

Bake under the broiler for 2–4 minutes until the sugar and cheese are caramelized. Sprinkle a pinch of sea salt on top. Serve on a clean plate with the port reduction as a sauce.

Note from Emily: To make this recipe super simple, you can finish it with a simple balsamic vinegar glaze from a store-bought bottle if you don't have time to make the port reduction.

Cauliflower Stew with Goat Cheese or Ġbejniet and Thyme (Recipe by Irene Borg)

I wanted to include this recipe because I saw it on Irene's kitchen table the day I went to visit her and her husband, Tony, to deliver the magazine issue in which he and I picked the prickly pears. She had just made this simple soup, and it looked so delicious that I could not stop thinking about it and I asked her for the recipe. It looks so simple and attractive in a bowl and makes a very satisfying meal when served with some Maltese bread or a ftira.

This is the recipe that Irene shared with me, without exact measurements. She is one of those who just knows what to do and puts it together to her preferred flavor and consistency. If you try this soup at home, less is more. Start with a small number of ingredients, like one single potato and just a few pieces of cauliflower and peas. There is a lot of liquid in this soup bowl.

INGREDIENTS
Onion
Garlic
Bacon
Maltese sausages
Potatoes
Peas
Cauliflower
Tomato paste
1 cube chicken stock
Salt and pepper
Red pepper flakes (if you want to add a bit of heat)

Goat or sheep cheese or ġbejniet
Orzo, rice, or any small pasta
Fresh thyme

INSTRUCTIONS

Fry onions, garlic, bacon, or Maltese sausages.

Add potatoes, peas, and cauliflower. Add a squirt of tomato paste and one cube of chicken stock, plus a pinch of salt and pepper. Cover with water and cook until soft.

Add ġbejniet or other fresh goat or sheep cheese after draining the cheese well. Simmer for five minutes and enjoy. You can also add orzo, rice, or any other small pasta. Garnish with fresh thyme for added flavor.

Chapter 7
You Deserve to Be the Breakout Star of Your Life

I grew up having a small mindset. I don't mean to sound disrespectful to anyone when I say that, but I did grow up always being afraid of pretty much everything and believing that I was never as good as all the people I was so often compared to. All my friends were smarter than me. All my friends were bound to become more successful than me. This is what I have always believed about my place in life. In turn, I created a life to support this belief. It wasn't until I was older that I started making friends who saw potential in me and encouraged me to think better of myself.

I have grown to surprise a lot of people from my past with the woman I am becoming, and whatever insecurities about myself that were still in me went to the wayside when I became a mother. Leading the way in the world for my own little women was the beginning of my path into the most sacred, expansive, and empowering opportunities for growth in my life. This is when I finally saw my reflection in the water and began to roar like the warrior lioness I never knew I always was. This is when I found my voice and embraced the new challenge of speaking up and being the advocate that my children needed me to be. I had to set the example and help nourish their pathway into becoming strong, resilient, confident women who are comfortable in their skin. It is an honor to be their mother and their guide. It is not possible to teach them well if I haven't done the work to impart the wisdom I am hoping to bestow upon them.

I recently had someone, a mother, messaging me asking all about how I managed to move internationally and what my life was like here for me and my family. When I started to tell her, she immediately wanted to move here as well. It's a predictable response. I am living basically in paradise. I am aware of that and so very grateful for it. She also went on to say something similar to the idea that I must have built up some serious karma to get this sort of reward. Maybe she's right. Maybe the years of struggle were building something bigger for me that I couldn't see. For such a long time, life felt like such a struggle. I know a lot of people who struggled their way through life and finally broke into a whole different phase of living that matched their true selves and allowed them to become bolder and more daring. I've seen a lot of people build themselves into something new from the ground up.

I've also known way too many people to count who are both brilliant and creative and did almost nothing with it. I've seen people run away from the potential and magic inside of them. I've seen others embrace the wildness and opportunity that they had inside themselves to expand and grab on to that goodness when it came. If you choose to play it safe, I completely understand making that decision. If you decide to go out on a limb and try something totally off the wall, I get that too. Should you decide to go for the latter, a few things are required to make it happen: the ability to dream it up, the smarts to figure out a way to make it happen, and the courage to follow it through. You are guaranteed to hear a lot of doubts radiating off everyone around you, but keep going. Be committed to your vision and trust that you have the goods to deliver. In Georgia, where I come from, we would say it requires some real *gumption*.

We all deserve the chance to be the breakout star of our own lives. We must choose to stop playing small. If our container is too tight, we must be willing to upgrade. We must find a larger container or break the mold altogether and decide there is no limit to what we can grow into! I don't want to live in a planter anymore. I want to be able to grow wild and free out in the fields. And for the first time in as long as I can remember, I am allowing myself to be limitless in what's possible. Every time I attach an outcome to something, I stop myself and decide that no numerological construct can be part of my inner dialogue as any sort of gauge of my efforts or rewards. I keep telling myself to *let it grow*, just like the farmers have taught me. Let it become whatever it is meant to become.

I have to be willing to stand back and trust the seeds I'm planting and let them grow wild. That is precisely when the containers break open and we breathe in and out in such a way that we can taste the freedom rising from within. Once you start to taste that freedom coming up from deep inside, there is no going back. Nothing else from the past will fit. You must become vigilant with your new self-expression and follow it through to wherever it may lead. Stop screwing the lids on the jars of possibility. Keep them open.

Growing Is a Pattern

Trees that bear fruit need a whole extra year to recover following a bountiful season. It takes a year of solitude and recovery for them to build their strength to do it all over again the following year. They still produce fruit in those down years, but in a much smaller capacity. The compelling part to think about is that even while they take their time to renew and begin to bloom again, something beautiful is always happening in the different phases of their growth. Those phases don't stop altogether; they just do a repeat cycle in a lesser form.

Take, for example, an orange tree. These trees grow ripe oranges during the winter months. After the oranges have finished their process and the remaining ones left on the trees have fallen off, you find beautiful white buds announcing themselves just a few weeks later. Then just a few weeks after that, the buds open up to make the most incredible-smelling orange blossoms. The bees come and visit, and it stays that way for several weeks. Then those blossoms disappear and all you see are green leaves everywhere and you wonder where the flowers went and where the new orange nuggets are. Before you know it, you spot little dark green babies growing in their place. Those little babies stay so small and green for so many months that it is easy to assume they are not going to grow this season. They stay in a state where they look like they're stuck until you simply stop paying attention to them. And then it happens—they get big and turn orange almost overnight. Remember, the very last thing to grow on a fruit tree is the actual fruit. So with timing, just as with growing, trust that the tree will bear fruit eventually, and so will you.

Even though they all go through the same yearly cycle, the trees yield more fruit every other year rather than every single year. Everyone, even the trees, needs downtime to prepare to go big again. Some of those trees in the field are on the same growth cycle and they bloom big together side by side. They were planted at the same time. The farmers are smart, though, and make sure they plant the other trees in the in-between years so that their big time to shine will be when the trees across the way are in their downtime. They time it just right so that everyone gets their turn to shine and everyone also has permission to rest after doing so.

The lemon trees here flower every full moon, totaling thirteen flowering growths per year. A friend of mine jokes that his lemon tree somehow missed the memo on when it was supposed to flower, so his tree only flowers on the lunar eclipse! He still loves his tree! My lemon tree might be exactly the opposite. I just noticed everything all at once on my lemon tree. I can see tiny bright green leaves of new growth along the branches, and there are lemon flowers still hanging on. There are both old lemons on the tree that are decaying, with black spots all over them, and brand-new lemons, bright and fresh, that we are using currently in our kitchen. It's all there—every single phase of growth making an appearance and letting me know that when the time is right, it all comes to fruition.

The lemon tree in my yard is showing me exactly what I'm trying to share with you: that we all deserve the chance to be the breakout star of our lives. Everyone has a time to shine, and everyone has a time to bear down and begin again. It's a cycle, and we need to honor the various phases we are in and honor the phases of those we love as they navigate their own growing patterns. Nothing can be in bloom all the time. It takes those in-between phases to prepare to grow and blossom.

Trust that even when you can't see it, you are always in one of those cycles of growth. You are always preparing for the next big surge in growth. Just as no one can be in bloom all the time, neither can anyone stay down without ever coming back up. It is the way of nature and all of life. Be ready for your next big cycle of growth and trust that you are already in it.

Olives: The Sweet, the Plenty, and the Sacred

I have become wildly curious about and fascinated with olive trees to make olive oil now that I live in a country where they are grown all over the island. The people from the surrounding Mediterranean countries are extremely protective and proud of the olives that their country produces. You cannot speak with a Greek person without being taught something about kalamata olives or being informed that Greek olive oil is the best in the world. Nothing compares to it. I have friends from Sicily who swear that that is the olive oil capital of the world. Then there is Tuscany, and let's not forget about Spain when we talk about olives! Since Malta is such a mix of so many expats from all over the surrounding areas, there is no shortage of people to ask and banter with about which olive oil is best and who you should buy your oil from and why.

Naturally, I set up an interview on olive oil to help me navigate my new curiosity-turned-passion. The one major takeaway for me after talking to several olive growers is that there is incredible olive oil from all around the world. There is no one best olive oil. There is only preference, and we need to learn about the specific varieties and which olives we prefer. That way, later on, we can blend our olives as we want to in order to create the flavor that we will love the most.

This might be the exact formula for life itself. No one is better than anyone else. We can start slowly and build our foundation into our knowledge base. From there, we can mix and match and play around to dial up or down the flavors of anything in life that brings us toward a place of pleasure.

The Mighty, Mighty Bidni

There is one olive in particular that I'm going to introduce to you that is native to Malta: the Bidni. These little olives have been proven by carbon dating to go back more than two thousand years to the Roman Empire. These olives from the small rural village of Bidnija have strong medicinal properties due to their high levels of polyphenols and low acid. They are supercharged and packed with both flavor and fervor. There is even research currently being done at the local university on the medicinal advantages of the Bidni olive in fighting illnesses because of the high levels of antioxidants and low levels of acid.

Here is the part where I introduce the concept that the mighty and the sacred many times find themselves not being as well known commercially as their counterparts. This is to say that the Bidni olive does not yet have a publicist and some of the other olives have had the spotlight for a great many years. The sweeter varieties of olives that are grown in other Mediterranean areas such as Tuscany, Sicily, Spain, and Greece yield much higher crops yearly per tree, and the olives, in general, taste sweeter. For this reason, many farmers have destroyed their Bidni olive trees and replaced them with imported olive trees that will offer more bang for the buck. It became all about the size of the olives and the amount of oil they produce rather than the medicinal properties of these sacred yet smaller jewels of the island.

Bidni olive trees are gifts from the gods, and they have been right under our noses for two thousand years waiting for someone who understood them to come along and shine a light on what they really are: powerful, magical, healing, and sacred among the trees. Even the trunks of this olive tree are a work of art. According to the Malta Independent, "A field of magnificent trees with huge trunks and intricate designs; a work of art in themselves, are found in the rural village of Bidnija."[22] I even managed to find a Bidni tree at a local organic ecovillage with a trunk that looks like two trees wrapped around each other, with arms and legs around the whole thing. It is stunning and intricate and makes any tree lover and olive lover stop and reflect on its immense and unique beauty.

Isn't that the case with so many things? Some things are so sacred and so powerful that it can be easy to dismiss them and overlook their value. That happens all the time to us when we play down the importance of our own lives. Each and every one of us matters greatly, whether anyone else recognizes it at first or not. Let yourself be seen. Allow yourself to be found. Trust that there is a place where your sacred gifts can shine brightly if you allow them to. It makes me sad that we gain confidence when someone else recognizes us and values our worth, but this is a way of life even among the olive trees. Now that the Bidni is gaining some traction, farmers are keeping these beautiful trees and starting to harvest the olives more and more. Who knows? Maybe soon enough they will get their very own publicity team backing them up and shouting their good name! Or maybe that new team has already arrived.

The Mediterranean Olive Oil Academy

Thanks to my new love affair with olive oil, I have made friends with the founders of the Mediterranean Olive Oil Academy. They work throughout the Mediterranean countries harvesting olives and making top-of-the-line olive oils. They sent me a bottle of the Bidni with hints of a pepper flavor that sticks to the back of your throat, as the Bidni is a very strong oil. They also sent one of the sweeter Italian oils, the Dolce di Rossano olive oil, where hints of almonds and artichokes are part of the flavor profile. They sent the two for me to learn to taste the difference between two such unique and different varieties of olives. Salvatore (one of the founders) even led me through a crash course on olive oil tasting over video before I tried either of the bottles they sent.

---

22. Malta Independent, "2,000-Year-Old Trees Still Producing Olives."

As with wine, when you add just a little bit of air into your mouth with the oil and mix the two, the flavor comes alive in your mouth. It's really impressive how different it tastes just opening up the sides of your mouth and inhaling while the oil sits on the tongue in the center of your mouth. This is when you can detect subtle notes of extra flavors, flower essences, or other aromatic hints that might go undetected if you just added the oil to bread and ate it. See what I mean when you put yourself out there? I wound up reaching out to the academy a week later and having a three-way zoom conversation with the founders, Dermott and Salvatore. People here are so generous with their time to help share their passion. It's such a treat!

At the Mediterranean Olive Oil Academy, they have made it their mission to introduce the Maltese Bidni olives to the world. And now, in this moment, I have become part of that mission. They want to teach about the value of these little healthy nuggets located right in our back-yard. They want to highlight the distinct aroma and taste of this extra virgin oil to the fullest. The olives are the star and the academy is now providing a stage for them. Finally, the Bidni has been discovered!

Olive Leaves

Trees that produce olives for eating are different from trees that produce olives for oil. The leaves from the trees are used in all sorts of healing and cleansing rituals. Olive oil leaves are often placed in pans and mixed with sea salt and sage, a sprig of fresh thyme, and even coal. Then the pan is lit and the smoke is wafted throughout the house to rid it of bad spirits. Every family has a slightly different recipe for what goes into the pan. On the Thursday following Palm Sunday, the leaves of the olive tree are blessed at the local churches, and for generations now, the grandmothers have taken those olive leaves home and burned them throughout the house to rid it of any curses or negative thoughts. I even have a bag of blessed olive leaves in my home that Doreen and Michelle made sure we all had.

People often take pieces of long candles (usually baptismal candles that have also been blessed) and add the olive leaves and sage and put it together in a bag, then place it in their homes for protection or in new cars to keep the car safe and protected. This is especially helpful if the car is new and people envy you for having something so nice. Being envied by people or being envious yourself is a character trait that is highly discouraged here. If the locals know that other people are feeling envious or possibly even jealous, they do a little zigzag with their fingers over their body or yours to help protect that energy from coming toward it. The finger position that I have seen is the index finger and pinkie extended, with the thumb, middle finger, and ring finger tucked inside (like the "rock on" hand symbol). From there, they take their right hand in this position and do a Z in front of their body from top to bottom to push the envy away from their space. As a general rule, Thursdays seem to be the common day to do practices like olive leaf burning, though I am unsure of the reason why.

We Grow to Our Prearranged Size

I have two olive trees planted so far, and neither one is a Bidni olive tree. I had never heard of it when I asked my gardener to find me olive trees to plant. When I asked him to find olive trees, he only asked me if I wanted olives to eat or olives to make oil with. I told him I wanted olives to make oil with. With that, he planted two Leccino olive trees imported from Italy.

Truth be told, I wanted to have my olive trees so I could go down to the fishing village where a local priest has an olive press and people bring their olives to him to turn into oil. I didn't necessarily care what kind of olives I could bring there, just that I was growing olives for my personal use. I had a very simplistic version in my uninformed mind about what olive tree growing would be. Following my big olive oil interview, I became more respectful of the whole process and began to look at every opportunity to interact with olive trees as something very intentional. I realized that I wanted to grow more olive varieties in my yard. With the quality of soil in this country, along with the weather, it is entirely possible to do so.

I began to survey our surrounding area and the space available to plant the trees in. You have to imagine the potential of what each tree could grow to be. You create in your mind the largest possible outcome for each one you plant, because you never know just how large or small a tree will become. When it comes to planting olive trees, the ideal spacing between trees is twenty feet. They need to be able to feel the sun on all their leaves and have their own space in order to grow to their full potential.

You see where I'm going with this, right? This is another thing that we have in common with the trees. We too need space in which to grow. We too need to bask in the full view of the sunlight. We too need nutrients to nourish ourselves fully. We too need good amounts of air and not too much wind. We too need enough space to grow so we don't have to compete with others trying to grow over us. We also need support for our roots to take hold and grow deep underneath to sustain the weather changes throughout the years. We also have no idea of the potential size we can grow into when we are placed in conditions to support our growth rather than suppress it. The next time you find yourself dreaming and making a plan for what is possible, think of the olive tree. Trust that you have everything it takes to manifest your dreams into reality.

We all grow to the size of the space that has been created for us. Therefore, it's only natural that we remain small when we are placed in a space that is made to keep us contained. Whether it's the containment that was created by expectations from outside ourselves or by the voices inside our own heads, we grow to the edges of whatever parameters we have been given. We remain small when we are told to believe that small is all that we *can* be. At each point of growth in our lives, we are faced with a choice once we are old and wise enough to jump spaces and find a plot that allows for uninhibited expansion, in the same way that a smaller tree planted in a pot will eventually need to be replanted in a garden or field if we want it to reach its full potential.

That little Bidni olive is smaller than the other olives that produce oil. It grows only half the size of something sweet like a Leccino olive. For more than two thousand years it has been a gift from the gods for its people, and its people turned the other way time and again simply because no one was educated on the power that these olives pack. But some of the trees remained, steadfast and mighty. Sometimes the most powerful of us are not seen until something around us finally recognizes the potential we have always had and shares us with the light. It is like the old story of the lion who grew up as a chicken and never knew she was a lion until someone took her to the water to see her reflection. Then she let out her first giant roar and never returned to the henhouse again. She became the lion she was born to be. Many times, more often than not, it takes some sort of outside reflection and recognition for us to realize that we were always the lion. Consider yourself recognized and do it yourself. You are the greatness within your reflection.

Spill It

If you want to speak in Mediterranean language terms, then this section is the olive oil of this book. In American terms, this is the meat and potatoes of this book. Here it is, the simple but harsh truth that may shake you up a bit, but I must say it. Here goes: We can no longer afford to blame any person, situation, or time in our lives for anything lacking in it. It is your responsibility and your absolute right to change the path and take your life by the reins. Direct yourself to where you want to be and stop making excuses why you can't. If that means getting counseling or therapy, taking medication, moving locations, quitting or getting your job, or going back to school, it is your responsibility to make it happen. This is a tough concept to digest, but it's important for me to express it in this very no-nonsense way to be sure there are no misunderstandings in the message.

You are so much more powerful than you may realize, and the opportunities that you might not see today have the potential to reveal themselves as you open up to them. I offer this information because when I was totally sideways in my own life and stuck in a downpour of severe anxiety and panic, I allowed way too many people to direct my path. I lost my sensibility of how powerful every choice I made really was. I gravitated to people who preferred to see me broken so that I would still need them and trust their opinions on matters regarding every aspect of my life above my own. Somewhere along the line, my voice became muted, both my inner voice and the one I used to communicate with the world around me. My basic trust of life and all the possibilities that come with it had gone into the deep recovery cycle of growth, and I completely lost my way.

I wish I would have understood sooner and more clearly that the power to heal, change, and grow has always been in my own hands. We hear it all the time that it always begins from within. However, I neglected to take personal responsibility for my health and healing, and it wasn't until I took back my power and began to fully trust my own inner wisdom that anything began to change. It took me many years, a lot of various therapies, and extensive personal work to gain control of my life.

I do not say this lightly that the power is yours. It is, but it was never meant to be you out there alone trying to figure it all out. There is support out there, but you must maintain your own voice and be the lead no matter who you allow in to help you. Once I got to taste life from the place of allowing all my instincts and inner knowing to lead the way, there was no turning back. I could taste that freedom rising. I tasted my power as it grew into something strong and bold. Once I started recognizing and savoring those new flavors of the delights that came with being in charge of my own very sacred life, there was no way I was going to allow anyone else's voice to control the narrative ever again. I broke the mold. It can never be restored, nor would I ever allow it to be.

Not everyone was on board with the new and updated version of me. Not everyone likes to see us evolve. Do it anyway. Not everyone likes to see us happy. Be happy anyway. Not everyone is comfortable with our newfound self-respect and boundaries. Boundary up anyway. Some people won't want to be in our lives anymore with all the new changes we have made. That part stings, I will not lie about that. It's tough to lose friends or lovers in our growing, but if they don't leave us first, we may eventually leave them because we have outgrown what isn't evolving too.

I only wish I could have understood this sooner! If I can help you by reminding you that you are so much more capable and resourceful than you may possibly realize, then that is what I want to do. Making any shift in our lives begins with a tiny droplet-size decision and then continuing to stand by that new decision, whatever it may be. Then you move into it. Begin by sticking with bite-size pieces to get you there. Go slowly and methodically through any of the jungles that you may feel like you are still trying to get through. Always come back to your center. Your center is your own inner wisdom, that gut reaction to every single stimulus that comes near you. Listen to it and honor it. There are always avenues that can lead the way to an elevated way of living your life, and you have the power to make it happen.

This has nothing at all to do with any change in location and everything to do with changes of the mind and your access to a higher level of happiness in your life. It has truly always been yours to decide how to use your sacred energy and power. Stay focused on the things you want for yourself rather than holding back and repeating all the reasons why things can never change. Then be willing to accept help from wherever it may come. Be honest with yourself and live from that space of total honesty and vulnerability.

Once we admit we need help in any way and open up to receiving the help, it creates an opening for new people to come and assist. Opportunities show themselves when we create the movement required to make the space that allows for them to happen. It is us who create the space for change, not things outside of ourselves. How they happen is totally out of our control, but the energy that attracts their existence is all within our own intentions and efforts. You are the one with the power to regain control over yourself and how ultimately you fit into your own life.

This doesn't have to be a whole life overhaul; it could be something as simple as making time each day to get outside and go for a walk or be alone in nature. Get your mind clear daily, and each day choose what you can do to make your day better than the one before. That alone will begin to change your life. I just don't want our own negative fear patterns and self-talk to convince us that we can't have something that nourishes our souls better. I cannot express this sentiment strongly enough. No one is going to come and save you but you.

If you want changes to come, you have to be the one to make them. If you are suffering from emotionally destructive patterns of thoughts and behaviors, I implore you to show yourself some grace and ask for help. While you must do your own personal work and that part does begin from the inside, it was never meant to be yours alone. Enter the community of help and support. Find a new place of belonging that accepts you for exactly who you are and where you are on your path. There is no shame in asking for help and being accepting of the help in whatever form it may come to you that garners results.

We live by way too many rules. If you are holistic, then you are not to touch medicine. If you are highly religious, then you are not to accept science. If you are emotionally distraught, then you are supposed to stay in that state of mind until it magically fixes itself. If you are exceptionally angry, then you are supposed to stew inside it until it explodes from the inside and you suffer at the cost of your mental, physical, and spiritual health. There does not have to be one way or the other. You are allowed to live in a "both/and" frame of mind and body. You can have your cake and you can eat it. And my goodness, you can enjoy every single bite as you go!

Food for Thought: Taking Your Power Back

During the different phases of our growing, there are bound to be moments when we are not nearly as in control of our lives as we'd like to think we are. There are times when we surround ourselves with people who prefer a more broken version of us because then they get to have control over us. This happens often in family dynamics with parents, siblings, children, and partners. It's easy to have someone else's voice be louder than our own. It also becomes easy to doubt our ability to have good judgment and decision-making skills when we have people around us who constantly question our ability to live in a healthy and balanced way. It's hard to see it when we are smack in the middle of it, but it becomes clearer and easier to recognize with each step we take in reclaiming our own sacred and healthy power. Becoming the breakout star of our own lives grants us permission to live freely in a more self-focused way and also more passionately. Here are some things to ponder:

- What is it that you need to be doing in order to become the healthiest version of yourself?
- Are there things you feel you need but have been hesitant to give yourself permission to pursue?
- Is there currently a need in your life to seek any sort of counseling or support, and if so, what is stopping you from getting it?
- Is there a desire to pursue other studies or enroll in classes of any kind? If so, which ones?
- What would it take for you to feel more balanced and empowered in your life?
- Are there certain relationships that you need to prioritize more or less for your emotional health and wellness?

If you answered yes to any of the above, sit with that and then figure out what has been holding you back and why. Remember that the choices you make are yours and yours alone. These questions and your answers to them especially should be kept private. It's your growth and your decisions, and you have the power to make them. Do not allow anyone else's voice to get in your head while you contemplate the next steps you want to take in your life. You deserve to live happy, healthy, wild, and free in a way that nourishes you deeply.

Food Tip and Recipe
by Jade Attard

Only when you get to experience staple pasta dishes like *spaghetti aglio e olio* can you fully understand the most important rule in Italian cooking: less is more. Having originated in Naples, *spaghetti aglio e olio* is a popular Italian dish made of only four ingredients.

This dish consists of some of the most essential ingredients in Italian (and Mediterranean) cooking: olive oil, garlic, spaghetti, and red pepper flakes. Considered a midnight snack by many, *spaghetti aglio e olio's* uniqueness is attributed to the fact that it is extremely easy to prepare with readily available ingredients you probably already have at home.

If you're in the mood for a typical Italian pasta dish you can prepare in around ten minutes, this recipe is for you.

Spaghetti Aglio e Olio
(Recipe by Jade Attard)

INGREDIENTS

1 package spaghetti pasta
8 garlic cloves, thinly sliced
½ cup (125 ml) extra virgin olive oil
½ teaspoon red pepper flakes (or more to your liking)

Additional variations:
Parmigiano Reggiano
Lemon zest/juice
Parsley

INSTRUCTIONS

1. Bring a large pot of water to a boil, then salt generously. Add the spaghetti and cook until *al dente*. To cook until *al dente*, test the pasta starting at two minutes before the suggested cooking time, which is usually 8 minutes.

2. While the pasta cooks, combine a generous amount of olive oil, minced garlic, and red pepper flakes in a large skillet over low medium heat. Cook for a few minutes until the garlic is lightly browned around the edges.

3. Reserve 4 tablespoons of pasta water before draining the spaghetti in a colander.

4. Add the pasta and pasta water to the oil and garlic mixture, mixing well. If using, add the Parmigiano Reggiano, lemon zest/juice, and/or parsley and keep stirring for another minute or two.

5. Serve and season with salt and pepper to taste.

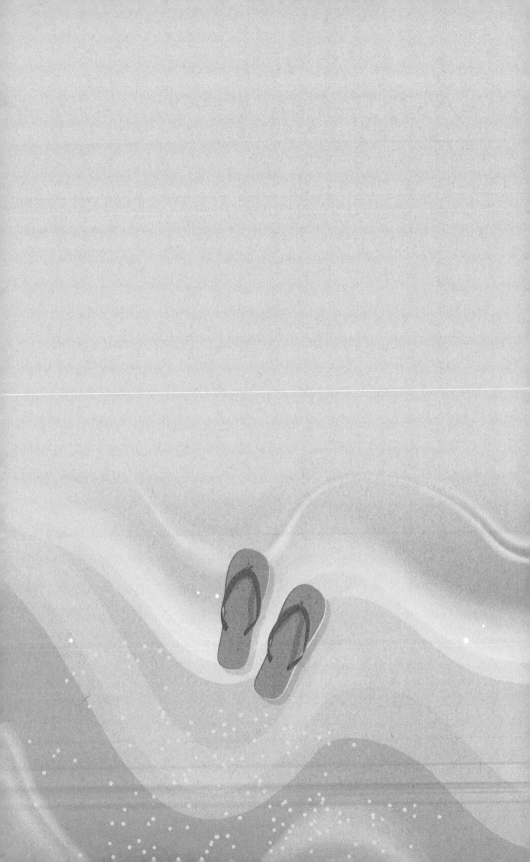

Chapter 8

Layer the Flavors

Combine all your life experiences. Integrate everything you have been with everything you are becoming. And then add some spice. If we do not learn to accept and even enjoy the various times of our lives for what they are, we will continue to waste perfectly good opportunities for pleasure. The pleasure body is real. Life is full of pleasures, should we allow ourselves to delight in them. The guilt has got to stop and we have to learn to loosen up on the reins a bit. Be simple, pure, sweet, spicy, and loving and learn to enjoy your life. Isn't that the dish we are trying to create?

Building Up on Flavors

There is an order to layering the flavors that will create the best main dish. Many chefs say that the difference between a good chef and a great chef is knowing not just what spices to add but when to add them. When you warm up spices, you start slowly to release their natural oils. This is the method to get the full-throttle flavor from an individual spice. You begin slowly and work with them to open up and let it all out. From there, you can choose to ground the spices or keep them in their original size and state.

Chef Guivisdalsky calls it "building up on flavors." He says that "in order for you to reach a greater flavor, or a greater sense for your palate, you must build up on one flavor after each other. If you want to use spices, you put them in the pan first to open them up to release their flavors into the pan. You can start by toasting the spice in the pan and then you remove them."

Chef Guivisdalsky also says that the pan is your base for your future flavor. He continues: "Let's say you brown your meat first and then remove the meat but keep that brown from the pan and the juices from the meat to build from. Then the vegetables, the same thing and then remove. Followed by a glaze if you choose to use a glaze with some liquids. Then you add each layer back in, bringing up all the flavors together during the stewing or simmering process."

Each flavor you add needs to be prepared as its own individual ingredient with its own special set of flavors. Every ingredient, be it a protein, vegetable, or spice, is removed after it is cooked and then put off to the side. The imprint from each one of those ingredients remains in the pan and creates your entire base for the dish that will be on your plate in the end, just as every experience of your life has helped to form a combination of flavors that remain at the bottom of the pan. Two things are happening here: the original action and the final combination of actions. And then there is a whole bunch in between to give it a healthy thickness and make it more fun. Everything in between serves an exact purpose. Everything you have ever done up until this point, and even what you have yet to do, all serve a very unique and specific purpose.

Just as the pan holds every layer as you go, so it is with all of life. All of our past experiences are always in the pan and the juices remain as the base that we build from. Then as each individual ingredient cooks, much the same way that we add individual new ingredients to our pan of life, the new flavors we add in help the dish become something unrecognizable from what it was when we started. It has become something else. All of a sudden, every layer and every ingredient no longer looks or tastes like any one of the single ingredients or layers. The dish has turned into something new and elevated, a complete meal. You can taste certain ingredients and notice the flavors that you like best, but as a complete dish, it is no longer any one thing.

The whole process of building up our flavors is exactly what we can do in life. We can add to them and turn them into something bolder, spicier, sweeter, zestier, even more bitter if that's where we want to go with it. It's our choice to make what we can with the ingredients we've got. Like the brilliant Theodore Roosevelt is often quoted as saying, "Do the best you can, with what you have, where you are." I say that to myself all the time. It's a simple truth to live by in life, in love, and in food.

Everything counts. Every layer was an important part of the creation of the dish that went into the making of who you are. But it cannot remain only a one-layer dish. Now it's a meal. And that meal doesn't look anything like it did starting out. It doesn't look like any one of the ingredients. It has become what it was designed to become. You are growing into what you were designed to become, too. Learn to utilize every single possibility and ingredient that you've been given. Every single person was born with something very unique and special inside them. We gravitate toward things that we find interesting and that we might be good at. It takes years for many of us to finally find things that we excel at and enjoy doing. Some know right away that they are gifted, and they run with it. With others, those gifts reveal themselves the deeper we go into our own interests and the more we learn about ourselves and how we want to spend our time.

For example, I've known people who struggled in school and never realized that they might be a more abstract thinker, which isn't in line with educational norms. Then they got to a certain age and were able to fully embrace the more creative side of themselves and found out they have a special knack for creating something that lines up with what they really want to be doing. This is when painters and musicians and designers emerge and people break away from the limits of old ways of thinking and teaching. This is also when we find out that trade schools may help us find that we are exceptionally skilled in a very specific area. The traditional primary education system limits a great many brilliant people. Not everyone has that mentor in their life who encourages them to break the mold and figure out on their own how they shine.

I am very set on this point because I was one of those people. Many times in life, finding self-confidence occurs once we find something that we are good at and really go after it. We find out that we are not lazy or ignorant and instead find out that we are actually very smart and disciplined and excel at the things that we had to discover on our own. What I remind my own children about on a daily basis, and what I will also say to you if you need to hear this, is that school or your level of education does not define how smart you are. You are smart, creative, brilliant, and capable. If your way of understanding the world around you does not match how others see it or the way it's been taught to you, know that your way is not wrong. It is different. And in the grand scheme of things, different often happens to translate into sheer and utter brilliance.

Your specific brilliance is exactly what can turn the dish you might be currently looking at from ordinary to extraordinary, and the seasoning spice is in the hands of your level of confidence to see yourself in a more capable way. Your job is to find out what it is that makes you come alive and then follow it into a place where you can make something with it. I know people who found out much later in life that they were very talented at painting. They ended up getting work painting bedroom walls in nurseries for families and became very much in demand. Others made their way to painting advertisements on buildings.

If you are good at something, never underestimate word-of-mouth marketing. I know people who make incredible jewelry and beautiful art. I also know people who found their confidence and stride when they went to school to become an electrician, a plumber, a baker, a makeup artist, or a hairstylist. The list goes on and on! Some people never went to school to discover their amazing talent, and that is wonderful too! It's in that process of self-discovery that you will find the most joy, no matter what road you take to get there. Just don't turn off that road. Let your work grow out of itself. "Let it ripen," as the farmers say.

Stick with what you love doing and don't give up on the idea that you have the power to turn it into a job, a hobby, a passion project, or whatever you want it to become. Will it into existence and then accept the help when it is offered to you to get it there. Start small and put everything you've got into each and every attempt at what you want to be doing. Your work becomes your signature.

When I use the term *work*, I do not mean a job necessarily, but rather our efforts and creations. When I use the term *my work*, I categorize it as my body of art, whether that is bodywork or writing or anything else I might be attempting to do. It is my work, my body of art and my own personal signature. You can call it whatever you feel most comfortable addressing it as, but for me, work means something much more than any job. You might be very surprised to discover that your specific skill set (so long as you cultivate the discipline needed to make it happen) is in demand somewhere. People too often settle for less, making the simple assumption that what they love to do won't translate into what pays the bills. That does not have to be the case. But you might have to get creative about how to turn it into a profitable venture if that is something you are after.

Brown Is Flavor, but Black Is Burned

One of the things that Chef Guivisdalsky teaches early on to his students is that when you brown something, it is flavor. If the pan is brown, that is not a bad thing; it's what we want. We are always trying to bring out the most flavor from any single ingredient of food, and brown is when you get it. With each level of browning, the flavors at the bottom of the pan begin their process of spilling out and presenting the possibility of adding themselves to everything to come. Then we allow all the flavors to mix and marry as we put all the ingredients together.

Should you lose your focus or get stuck on one part for too long, that beautiful brown color will quickly turn to black and the taste will be burned. Some things take only a mere moment to expose their flavor, and other items might need to simmer a bit. You have to get to know every ingredient you are working with and how to help each one of them reach their maximum potential.

When we talk about layering the flavors as a metaphor for life, we need to use our experiences as well as our dreams to build on each other. Some of our layers haven't even happened to us yet, but we are planning for them to be used and so we gather and set out all the ingredients to have ready, meaning we prepare ourselves and work on ourselves so that all of our specific skills can be put into motion when the time comes. That way, when the opportunity presents itself and it's time to use our skills, we can. Some ingredients of our lives we cook up and set aside knowing they are part of our dish but won't be added in until the timing is right, while other things we may burn and need to throw out. Everything we absorb from the world around us is shaping us and serving some sort of purpose that we might not yet be able to see. Sometimes we can't know what that specific purpose will be for quite a while, until it shows itself to us.

We must trust that every aspect of ourselves that we work on and help to grow and enhance, even every pitfall we run into, is all leading us to someplace else. Keep going. Keep gathering the tools and the support that you will need in the future. Create better things now so that one day you can look back on all the work you did and recognize that it is exactly what got you here. Do it with intention. Creating a recipe for our lives that will feed our souls does not need to include painful memories and spices that burn. It's a new dish we are creating, and though everything we have experienced has had a hand in shaping who we are, we no longer need to be defined by any of them. We choose what layers to add back in to our new dish for a second round. We can't erase the first coating, but we can choose not to put something back in again when we layer the new flavors. We choose what the flavor profile will be. We decide if we want it spicy with heat or spicy with flavor or mild through and through.

We are creating ourselves in a new way and using all the ingredients that we decide will make their way into our dish. But one thing to keep in mind is that although we might be excited to play and experiment with certain spices, not all of them will get along as a combined dish. We must be clear about what we are trying to create and what ingredients should be added to make that dish. Many tragedies have happened to any one of us in our lives. There are lots of ingredients that I would never consciously choose to keep at the bottom of my pan. Some of the hard times will always be there and will always remain part of my story. In life, it is always important to tend to any traumas and process them head-on so that they don't continue to weigh you down. I don't want to offer a layer of toxic positivity here, where we dismiss negative thoughts and feelings or offer false assurances rather than being comfortable with the burned parts.

The point I am making is that the parts of life that were traumatic, and that we have taken steps to work through so that they don't continue to be so weighty, don't serve a good enough purpose to add them back in for our second round of flavoring. It's not blissful ignorance; it is awareness and intention of what we want to add to our next new plate. I personally would not be exactly where I am now without all the hardships I had to work through, but I am not any one of them as a single ingredient, and neither are you. Some of those rancid ingredients have no purpose in the next dish. Food is life. You can always figure your way through to just the right recipe for what you want for your next dish.

We are creating each of the layers of flavor intentionally. If you burn your dish, you don't set the burned pieces aside only to add them back in to the other layers that you've cooked correctly! What would be the point in purposely ruining your next plate of food? When we burn something, we have no choice but to throw it out and clean the pan so that we can start over with what ingredients we have left and make something new out of them. Then we start again with whatever extra ingredients we may have on hand as we create a new and possibly slightly different plate than we had originally planned. Sometimes those dishes turn out to be the *winner winner chicken dinner* plates anyway. You just never know what it will be until it gets made! That is exactly what I am trying to get us all to do in creating something more flavorful and wonderful for ourselves with our lives! At some point, we have to be willing to throw out the burnt parts! They serve little purpose except to teach us what not to do the next time.

The Outliers

Nothing in life is a level playing field. Many will have to work much harder than others to achieve the same goal. That is an honest fact of life that should never detour us from going after something. Just because it doesn't seem that we have been set up to get it the way other people seem to does not mean that it's not a possibility for us. I have given much thought to the idea that certain destinies seem to have been written in the stars, while others seem to be lost so much of the way. Some people know exactly what they want to do with their lives and then create everything they can do to support that dream. Others bloom later and maybe stumble around for what seems like a very long time before they find a good place to land.

Sometimes I think about movie stars and how it seems like they were born to shine. Most celebrities were born with some sort of specific something that helped to make them the known entities that they have become, such as looks, talent, and family ties. Some were born into the industry and had the connections that other people could never get no matter how many years of effort they put in. To the outside world, it might look like the opportunities were handed to them on a platter. But even if you are born into a direct line to success, you still have to do the work. Even the most famous actor's children still have to start by attending acting lessons. No one walks in and becomes great at anything without a massive amount of effort behind it. Anything that looks like it didn't take effort usually required the most grueling practices to make it look that way behind the scenes.

Even writing a book requires an unbelievable amount of work for years and a ton of patience to make it happen. Every time I'm in the deepest and most difficult process of editing, I remind myself of one simple truth: in the end, it's supposed to look like it was easy. No one else needs to see how much blood, sweat, and tears went into it. They just need to see the finished product and make their own assumptions. As with any gourmet dish, we have no idea how much time it took to create a dish so full of layers of flavors. In the end, it may look and taste like a simple and flavorful dish, but the effort it took to be created may far exceed any of our imaginings. The only part we think about is how good it tastes, not what it took to make it. That is the markings of true success: it was supposed to look easy.

It takes years of effort to become an overnight success. Constant practice, an eye on the target that never wavers, and the discipline to see it through are required of anyone who takes on such an incredible invitation into that way of life. But there are so many people we see who are hugely successful and we make the assumption that they somehow won the cosmic lottery and that it all came quickly, easily, and with minimal effort. As author Mike Dooley once said, "The one thing all famous authors, world-class athletes, business tycoons, singers, actors, and celebrated achievers in any field have in common is that they all began their journeys when they were none of these things."[23] I keep that quote on my refrigerator to remind myself that I have just as much potential as anyone else to do something special with my life. I hope it reminds you of the same. We all have a specific purpose and skill set beyond what we might have been told we have. We all have that magic ingredient. It is up to us to discover what that is.

I have always felt inspired by this quote, but now I see it just a little bit differently. They may have begun when they were none of these things, but for many people, where they are located will make a huge difference in the availability of something being attained. If I went into greater detail about my life here in Malta and how surreal my sliding into a dream life really looked, it would seem that I have become one of life's outliers. At least it feels like that to me. I didn't do anything specific to deserve it, but I took every opportunity it afforded me and I ran with it.

---

23. Dooley, *Manifesting Change*, 195.

I will share this little part because it is a very accurate comparison and does give one something to think about in terms of location and availability. I have been writing books for the last at least fifteen years. I have clawed my way into finally getting professionally published after years of grueling effort. Still, not many people know my name and my television appearances have been maybe two locally and a few lucky strikes along the way for totally random things. Even paying a fortune for a publicist with my previous book and doing more interviews than I ever had, I had zero television appearances, though we pitched to all of them. Now that I live in Malta, a tiny island where people want to connect me to their friends who host television shows or anything else they can help me with, I have already been a guest on a local wellness show on their Saturday primetime media channel over twenty times over the course of the last two seasons. More than twenty times! I also appeared on one of the most-watched television shows and am writing for a major local magazine. I've even been recognized here—more than once!

When I tried to do any of this in the US, it felt like I was begging for any attention at all, for anyone to see that I had something valuable to share. I am the exact same person now, except I love this place and people really enjoy experiencing their sacred home through my eyes. I am now conveniently placed in a prime spot with regard to both location and connections that are making this all possible. I had neither of those things before. The landscape in which I am trying to build my brand has completely changed. I am acutely aware of how rare this opportunity is that I have been given, and I am in no way trying to say that anyone else would have the same result even if they followed the same game plan. It also depends on what lens a person is looking through as far as what a dream life looks like for them.

What I have is pure gratitude for what has been afforded to me through this life-changing process. I try not to take for granted how very different my life is over here. So maybe I am an outlier now. What is an outlier you may ask? According to the *Cambridge Dictionary*, the definition of an outlier is "a person, thing, or fact that is very different from other people, things, or facts, so that it cannot be used to draw general conclusions."[24]

Like most people in the free world, I watch a lot of videos. I came across an old friend a few years ago who posted several videos that caught my attention. I found myself following this person over the years for one reason: her son. Don't take that to sound as creepy as it appears in writing. I love watching the videos she posts of her son doing trick moves on the ski slopes. Her son was born and raised in a snowy Colorado town, and one day his mom posted a video of him skiing at his ski school that he goes to every day. Wait…ski school? I was in awe immediately, realizing that this kid would get to grow up on the ski slopes. It won't be a yearly or every-few-years vacation for him; it will be his life. I thought to myself, "That kid is so lucky! He probably has no idea how lucky he is that he gets to grow up in that kind of life. I wish I could do something cool like that for my kids." Obviously, I was not yet living in Malta when my wishes for such things had begun.

The truth is, I do not love the snow, I hate the cold, and I can't ski. This story is not an exact parallel of what I hoped for myself specifically, but it struck a chord in me. I checked this woman's page often just to see if there were more videos. This sort of life setup reminds me of the work of Malcolm Gladwell. In his 2008 book *Outliers*, Gladwell studied the many ultrasuccessful people who had more opportunities than practically anyone else in their respective fields. None of the odds seemed to be stacked against them. Instead, all the odds were in their favor: "Virtually all the big names of the IT industry—Steve Jobs, Steve Ballmer, Scott McNealy, Eric Schmidt—…were born between 1954 and 1956. Those dates are crucial. Any older, and upon graduating they'd have been hoovered up by the likes of IBM and trapped into the mainframe way of thinking."[25] Furthermore, "one of Gladwell's key arguments is that raw

---

24. *Cambridge Dictionary*, s.v. "outlier," accessed August 2022. https://dictionary.cambridge .org/dictionary/english/outlier.

25. Danton, "What Do Bill Gates, Steve Jobs and Scott McNealy Have in Common? They're Lucky."

ability and hard work aren't enough. You need to be born at the right time and then have the right opportunity."[26]

I've talked about timing before in this book. Like relationships that are 10 percent attraction and 90 percent timing, so too is the timing of an outlier in terms of age, location, and opportunity. Gates, Jobs, and the others weren't just born in one of those crucial years; they were also all raised in or near Silicon Valley. This is significant information to understand how they came to be some of the biggest outliers of our time. They were in exactly the right place at the right time, and they took full advantage of the opportunities afforded to them because of this. They are also creative geniuses who work morning, night, and day. Their work ethic is not common. All of these things create an outlier. This doesn't necessarily mean that they are or were smarter than other young tech enthusiasts, but with the right combination of time when you were born, availability of what it is you want to be doing, hard work, and sheer luck, one can break out of the mold of the norm and reach a height that few others in the world will be able to. This is the outlier. This is something extremely rare and all the conditions have to line up almost exactly. These are not normal circumstances.

It also does not mean that only those people have an opportunity to be the great success story of their time. Besides, what the term *success* means varies wildly from person to person. For me, feeding your soul does not have anything to do with the numbers on any scale; it has to do with finding an exorbitant amount of personal peace and happiness in your life. No one can measure that from any person to another. That is the recipe I want us to work from.

But I also think some of these people are wonderful examples of what is possible in the world. Circumstances, chance, location, and luck are always at play for any one of us at every turn. The playing field is never level, but I still believe that where you live in relation to your dreams and passions plays a huge part in making them come true. Wishing to pursue

---

26. Danton, "What Do Bill Gates, Steve Jobs and Scott McNealy Have in Common? They're Lucky."

skiing as a sport but living nowhere near snow is a nonstarter. At some point you will need to ask yourself where you need to be and what things you are willing to trade in order to get there. But this applies only to the goals that are out of the norm. You can be successful at anything you put your mind to. It's a matter of discipline, focus, unwavering dedication, passion, and perseverance. Keep your focus there if you want to make something happen. Then trust that there is a plan for you and go for it all the way.

I was born in Southern California right in the heart of Los Angeles. My dad loved living in LA, but my mom got homesick and made him take us all back to Ohio. I was only three at the time. I spent a lifetime wondering what my life could have been like if I had grown up in Tinseltown. Would I have been a stunt double? Would I have been famous? Would I have done loads of drugs and cut out early? I will never know what that pathway would have looked like.

When I finally visited LA for the very first time, I was twenty-three and immediately felt like I was home. I made friends I kept in contact with for years, and we would visit each other in Atlanta and LA. I would go to LA at least once a year. I loved it there, but it wasn't my home and I never made the brave jump to make it that way. I always told myself that I couldn't afford it. Now I know better. I make a lot more money when I'm fully invested in making something happen, and the universe has always backed me up on that. Money has never been my biggest priority, but whatever I've needed to make happen, I've always found a way to pull it off. When you really want something and you put everything you have behind it, you can find a way to make at least part of it come true. Of course, this would be the opposite of an outlier. This is daydreaming at its finest.

I have a few friends who moved to LA to make their dreams come true. I admire those who went for it. I have several friends who did make LA their home and stayed there for many years trying to make something of themselves. Some are still there doing incredible things and taking full advantage of life's incredible opportunities. I love it when I see them on

TV or in a movie. I am so proud of them and their bravery to go after it. I love watching anyone knock it out of the park. There are opportunities in California, and in Hollywood especially, that practically no other place in the world can offer. The whole town has been built upon the collective dreams of many bold and brave people who made it their home. Meanwhile, on the other side of the world, someone else was creating a Hollywood experience for their people. "After early Indian experiments in silent film, in 1934, Bombay Talkies, launched by Himansu Rai, spearheaded the growth of Indian cinema."[27] Over the years, several classic genres emerged from Bollywood.

Though Hollywood, California, is not the only place to make your dreams come true, there are only a few places in the entire world where your chances of success in that industry increase monumentally. Malta is now being dubbed the "Hollywood of the Mediterranean" because it has become home to major motion pictures over the years and continues to build into a massive hub for the film industry. Maybe they will label it Maltiwood!

In many cases, it may be true that where you are in the world highly increases or decreases your chances of hitting it out of whatever park you are aiming to play in. Famous athletes leave their families at a very young age to live and train with their coaches if they have their sights on the Olympics or something near that level. You might have to be willing to give up almost everything in pursuit of your dream. That is just the deal. Musicians move from all around the world to make it in New York, California, or Nashville. You have to put yourself in the location where your dreams have a chance to hit. Or perhaps you are lucky enough to already be living in a place where other people would have to give up their lives to go and stay to make it happen. That's one of the things that puts you in a unique position to be one of life's outliers.

27. Ians, "The Enigmatic Indian Film Industry & Its Expansive Reach."

Beyond Location

Most people say the goal is to create peace within and then the rest of the world around us will somehow follow suit. That makes it sound like the outside world is somehow less important. I disagree with this. I believe that while our internal environment is the most valuable asset to living peacefully, it is not the only part that lends to the experience of elevated levels beyond contentment. I believe that everything we are surrounded with will bring us closer to or further away from gaining an experience of happy, joy, and bliss that is beyond any singular aspect.

Where you are within yourself, regardless of location, plays an enormous role in creating the life of your dreams. You have to be watchful that no matter where you are, those you team up with and place around you will determine your probability of success in any given area. It can support or destroy everything you have ever worked for in your life. This is why many addicts are encouraged to move away from the only home they have ever known in order to maintain sobriety. The place you built your life around may or may not be the best thing for you. The people in it may or may not be the people you need for your soul's evolution. This is important to take notice of as well.

Everyone you surround yourself with is a reflection of yourself. Some of those people are vitally important to your growth and evolution. They support everything you do and encourage you to be the best version of yourself. Others will go out of their way to tear you down, because they like the broken version better than someone strong and resilient. Every single decision you make adds a layer to your pan. Every important person in your life creates the side dishes for your main course. Do they match the theme of the next courses in your life? Sometimes you will need to set out on a new path and collect new friends, new lovers, or new habits and behaviors that lead you to the dessert portion of your life's meal. Collecting new people does not imply that you must release the others who came with you, but you may need to rearrange where they sit at your table. No one can make those choices for you.

The *Ping*

Have you ever paid attention to your instant reaction whenever you travel to any new place? You could be in the same state, like Florida perhaps, and feel immediately at home by one body of water and instantly repelled by another. There are places all over the world that stimulate either an *at home* response or a feeling that *this place is not for me.*

I know of people who have visited places like Hawaii and immediately came home and started searching the want ads to find a way back there. They loved who they were in a place like that. They loved how that place made them feel. They loved the view and the vibe of that area. I had a friend who went on a vacation to a healing center once and cried on the airplane all the way home because she felt so at peace in that location. She couldn't shake it. She also couldn't up and move there, so she figured out a way to insert herself into that center where she would become a guest presenter on a yearly visit. This is what I describe as the *ping*. It's almost as if a little bell rings inside us or we feel like we are being poked when we meet people or visit places that are in alignment with us.

Once you get that internal *ping*, if you listen and don't allow the time between your initial introduction and the next to put you off while you talk it down as a silly pipe dream, there can be a way to get yourself into that place, even if simply on a visiting basis. That inner *ping* is something you feel instantly. It's a feeling we get when we know that we are in a place that we are meant to visit again. What is it about various places around the world that make you feel such a pull or push? Can you classify it? It's the same feeling we get with people. We know right away when we meet someone who feels like home or who feels like an opposing magnetic force. If you listen to your body's response to people and places long enough, it will become your guiding force of wisdom. It's a feeling you can't shake and something important to pay attention to. Your body always knows the way. Trust it.

Astrocartography

Astrocartography is an astrological system where the exact time, location, and date of birth is believed to help create the path you are meant to take in this life. Astrocartography is a method that matches your natal chart with the demographics around the world.[28] This implies that there are places around the world where your energy may run higher or lower. Some people use this system to plan vacations or make moves that may be advantageous.

It's funny that I have been incredibly fascinated by this system, yet I have never had my birth chart done or even met anyone who knows how to do it. The concept of astrocartography alone means a great deal to me, because I believe in it more than ever before. Without a doubt and no matter what any person or chart could tell me, I know that Malta was always a place my soul was meant to experience. It's been waiting for me to find my way here. It feels like home to me. It has from the moment I arrived. I can honestly say that I feel like I live an extraordinary life here. I am a very different person coming through this experience, one whom I like better than ever before. The people I have met in Malta, the life I have created here—it could not have been done without exactly the way that everything unfolded here. It also encouraged me to become braver and put myself out there with the trust that it would not all be in vain. My life is not normal here. It is elevated in a way that feels divinely orchestrated.

Food for Thought: Creating Your Own Recipe

In layering the flavors of yourself into your own dish, how would you create a recipe that reflects the layers you've already put into your pan? What are the current layers? What are the layers you are hoping to add? Stick to keywords for this exercise. I usually shy away from using identifiers to describe ourselves, but in this case, short and to the point offers

---

28. Brown, "Astrocartography Is the Key to Planning Dream Vacations and Making Fulfilling Moves."

enough description for you to remember who you were, what you are working with currently, and what you are planning to add in as a way to layer your own flavors and create a solid recipe for your life.

For example, there are things I used to be, like gymnast, cheerleader, athletic instructor, and schoolteacher, with a pinch of happy that always went in with those things. Those are past key terms that would describe the most prominent layers that were first thrown into my dish. Then there are the current layers, which might look more like mother, wife, writer, animal lover, and my favorite spice to work with currently: a dash of joy. Then I have the layers I'm preparing to add to my dish. They might be something like world traveler, award-winning and best-selling author, and screenwriter, with a hefty shake of brave, luck, and bliss as my spices. Those are layers I'm hoping to add.

I have my past, my present, and my hope for the future in my dish as layers of flavors. Keep in mind that I could have thrown in exactly the opposite to the words I chose for my dish. Life has not always been so good to me, and I have not always been so good to myself. But for the recipe I want to add to, I'm focused on the positive side. This does not in any way mean that you have to. You can create the recipe in whatever stance you are currently mixing from. Be honest and also be fair. This is just an exercise for you to see the points of interest that stand out the strongest to you. It's an interesting exercise to do, and from day to day, as your recipe may change. Some days it's mush and other days it's dessert.

Now it's your turn to layer your flavors. What keywords describe the main points of focus for your childhood, adolescence, and early adulthood? Then what keywords would you use to describe your life's recipe currently? What are you playing with right now in your life? Follow this with either the ingredients you already have set out in front of you to add in or the ingredients you are still working on harvesting to add. Then you have your specifically layered dish. From there, you can be a bit introspective and see what words came to you that were positive and what words came to you that felt heavier to your heart and soul. This is your recipe and your specific dish. Even if some of the bottom has some burnt parts, you can always add in more of the good stuff to even it out into something more pleasing to your soul. It's not over yet, my friend. Add that spice and make something delish with what you've got. You are the chef in this kitchen.

Food Tip and Recipe

This is a recipe I was given when I took that course on how to spice up your salads at the Mediterranean Culinary Academy. I put it in this chapter because it's a simple chicken dish that anyone can make. However, when you spice it up and taste the incredible spices mixed in with the Greek yogurt, it takes on a very elevated flavor.

This chicken becomes something scrumptious when you throw in every layer of flavor. Start with something simple and notice that everything and everyone has the potential to kick it up a few notches, and this includes you.

Yogurt Marinated Chicken
(Recipe by Ariel Guivisdalsky)

INGREDIENTS
Chicken leg deboned, 1 per serving
40 grams (3 tablespoons) yogurt
1 clove garlic, minced
1 teaspoon smoked paprika
1 teaspoon ground cumin
1 teaspoon ground coriander
½ teaspoon dried chili, crushed
Salt to taste
1 tablespoon olive oil

DIRECTIONS
1. Begin by combining the yogurt, garlic, spices, and salt in a mixing bowl.
2. Add the chicken to the bowl and coat evenly in the marinade.

3. Allow to sit in the fridge for up to 12 hours or leave at room temperature if you are going to cook shortly.

4. Heat a sauté pan over medium-high heat and place a sheet of parchment paper in the pan if it is not nonstick to prevent the food from sticking (and also because it makes for easy clean-up) .

5. Add a tablespoon of olive oil to the pan and allow to heat for one minute.

6. Lay the chicken in the pan away from you and allow to cook 3–4 minutes on each side until well browned.

7. Finish cooking the chicken in the oven if necessary. Check for doneness by touch or by using a probe thermometer and look for a reading of 165°F (74°C).

8. Allow the chicken to rest for a few minutes before slicing and serving. Add more salt to the sliced chicken if you prefer heavier seasoning.

A Simple Side

Steamed Broccoli, Cauliflower, or Romanesco with Olive Oil (Recipe by Salvatore Romano)

Salvatore, one of the founders of the Mediterranean Olive Oil Academy, offered this super simple recipe to enhance the flavor of vegetables during our video call the first time we met. I'm always looking for simple ideas that can entice my children to try new things. He offered this as an idea, and it has been a hit in our home.

Begin by taking a head of broccoli, cauliflower, or Romanesco broccoli and steam it until it's soft to your preference. Once it's cooked and off the heat, sprinkle with sea salt and pour a bit more than a drizzle of olive oil over the full head. When it comes to extra virgin olive oil, it can be cooked with but should not be used for frying. It is the type of oil to finish a dish with. You can pour it over the vegetable when it's warm, but avoid doing so immediately after taking it off the heat. Give the vegetable a minute or two to cool down and then finish with the salt and oil.

Even my children enjoy their broccoli, cauliflower, and Romanesco more when I prepare it this way. It is not oily or even salty. It just tastes like your vegetable is a little bit more lively and happier as it comes in for the party that will soon be happening in your mouth!

The Dessert Menu

"If you are more fortunate than others,
it's better to build a longer table, not a higher fence."
—Anonymous

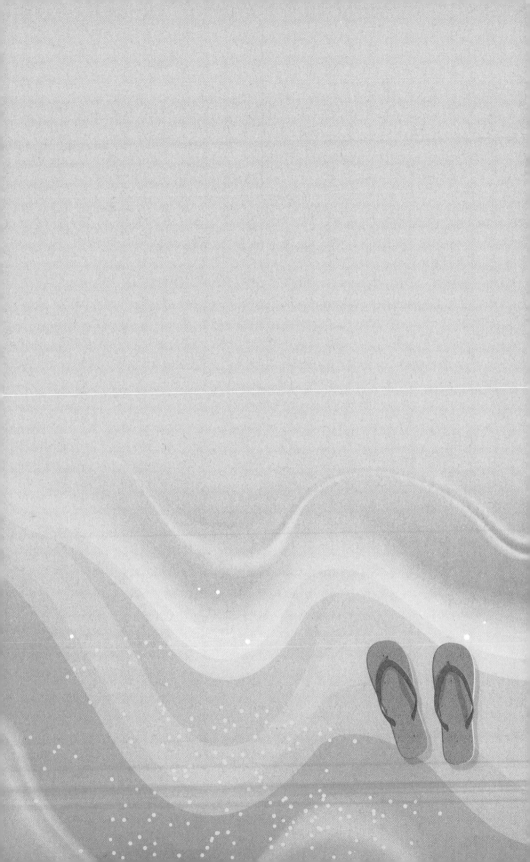

Chapter 9
Count Your Blessings

Blessings are everywhere in the world. Some might be harder to recognize, but they never leave you completely. There is always something to be grateful for, but I am not asking you to forget the reality of the difficulties that life will surely present. Just as blessings abound, so too does strife. In between the highs and the lows, there is a sacred place to go to keep you from feeling dizzy. That place is in the silence. Some call it the void. Others call it the stillness. It is a sacred place that we have to consciously put ourselves into in order to harmonize ourselves with that gentle flow of the universe.

Some call this practice prayer, centering, centering prayer, meditation, or contemplation. I like to think of it a little bit more simply, without using a specific title, and instead just think of it as allowing myself into the flow of the silence that the universe always has available to us. It is always out there, always available to us, and the best thing we can do is learn to drop ourselves into that consciousness when we need to be there. Think of it like different sound waves, and one of them is peacefully silent. We want to find that layer and slip into it when we need to. It's a place of perfect peace. Try not to overthink it or attach it to a specific name of a practice. It is simply a drop-down of our conscious awareness into the space within the universe that sits in stillness. It's always open for you to visit when you want to.

Be Still

The Hebrew root of the words *be still* does not translate to "be quiet." It translates into the idea of "let go." The faith in Malta is very deep and extremely personal. The idea behind the statement *Be still and know that I am God* translates toward the notion of *Let go and know.* Let go of trying to control every narrative around you. Focus on your faith and your own good life and spend time dwelling within your soul instead of trying to get anyone to believe whatever you believe. Out here in Malta, at least among the people I have met, there are no discussions of trying to convert anyone to any kind of faith practice. Instead, they work on their own and they shape it as they go. This is such a breath of fresh air to me.

A church does not necessarily equate to faith, but it does offer a place to go when you need more of it. Tons of people pray, meditate, and live their daily life through a deep sense of faith, and you may or may not ever see them at any given house of worship. You will find me in many churches along these islands, but it likely won't be when others have gathered. My faith is my own and I celebrate it through how it feels in my soul. You don't have to go to church to allow the Great Spirit into your heart. It's not a weekly event, but rather a constant. Here in Malta, the country is 98 percent Catholic. It is much like Italy and Spain that way.

Anywhere you go in Malta, you will find a statue of Mary, Jesus, or the saints. They hide in plain sight at the front and back of almost every home or building. If any statue of a religious nature is built into the stone of a building, it is considered protected and cannot be knocked down even under new ownership. Giant statues sit at street corners and in the center of roundabouts. They are carved into buildings and sit atop or in front of them. Next to almost every single door on the front of every home is some sort of religious relic embedded into the building itself.

The people of Malta don't do this because they are trying to flaunt their religious status. They do it as part of a practice of faith and as a sense of protection that their homes will be guarded by the Blessed Mother or a particular angel or saint. There are 359 Catholic churches on the islands of Malta and Gozo. From tiny chapels along the farm roads to large intricate churches with paintings from floor to ceiling that resemble small versions of the Sistine chapel, they are everywhere on this island. If you wanted to go church hopping, you could almost do a different place for every day of the year.

This country is filled with a rich history drenched in faith. You can feel the history of the years of prayer like an umbrella that hovers over the entire island. I have never experienced this feeling of being so divinely protected as I have felt living here. I also feel surprisingly free of judgment here. Here, a strong faith is something very personal, and they recognize that and respect it. No one asks you if you attended church this Sunday. No one goes out of their way to make you feel bad if you do or do not attend a service. It's not their business. They stick to the idea that their faith practice is their own and your faith practice is your own and leave it at that. It is not their place to save you, judge you, or convert you.

Yet, conversations about prayer happen so easily in the context of what people are thankful for. It feels as if the community all prays for similar outcomes, such as rain for the farmers, plants, animals, etc. There are always conversations about faith and prayer, but it's more externally driven. For example, "Pray for rain!" The word *you* tends not to be included in prayer statements here. It's a small distinction, but one I have most certainly picked up on and appreciate very much. Everyone does it their way here. No one asks what your practice looks like. There is freedom here to find your faith and forge your relationship with your Creator, which allows people to explore their own pathways into their faith.

Who Are You Called to Be?

There is an anonymous quote I read years ago that hit me hard when I read it and that I've never forgotten: "Someone once told me the definition of Hell: The last day you have on earth, the person you became will meet the person you could have become." Think about that. There are so many things we could have become, but we chose to go another way. Can you imagine the moment when you see where every path you didn't take would have led? Some would be amazing, while others could have been our complete destruction. Not all paths we didn't take would have led to something bigger or better. With change comes a million fears. When we think of the missed opportunities that were presented to us for that growth, it can taste bitter minus the sweet. It can be worse than the fears we felt before we chose which move to make or skip.

I am not asking you to move. I am asking you to listen deeply to whatever is calling to you and follow it as you are able. If you were not wishing for at least some part of your life to expand, you probably would not have picked up this book. In recent world history, there is nothing I can name that has been a bigger wake-up call than the pandemic to show us that life is short, precious, and fragile. I don't want to miss out on what could have been. I don't want you to either. Joy is real and it is felt in the body, mind, and soul. It is not specific to any one person, place, or thing. It is available to anyone who is willing to taste it and feel it. Take it in when it comes and do not push it away. Savor it when it shows itself to you. Sit still inside it when you feel its presence and soak it up. Make friends with the experience of joy. Make it a more constant part of your life. Joy is so entangled with gratitude that when one comes to you, the other one is likely to follow closely behind. Let them intermingle, and allow yourself to take it all in.

The path of growth and acceptance of our true self will cost us the life we are living with now and many of the relationships in it. You might be working hard to fit into a space that was always too small and try to make it work. When life is lived simply by default and not through your own hands and choices, be assured that some sort of personal discord will surely follow. I've been that person. I've lived much of my life as if it was mismatched. I've had the heart of the daydreamer who never had the guts to follow it through.

I left a few times in search of that something bigger and bolder, but I always ran back home before things could develop into something more interesting. I have experienced that inner knowing that I was stuck in places because I was too afraid to create something else. I knew I wanted more but had no idea how to make any of it happen. I know what it feels like to try to be something that I was never designed to be in order to fit inside a box that was always too tight to fit. I know what it's like to suffer from deep anxiety and life-blocking fear and hide from any sort of real living. I know it so intimately that I can easily recognize it when I see it in someone else. I also know (and not just because of this move to the Mediterranean), because of deep and extensive personal growth and a reclaiming of my life as a whole, what it feels like to finally go free.

Go Free!

When my children were babies and could not yet walk down the stairs, we had our three dogs expertly trained to sit at the top in the *stay* position and wait until both children turned around backward and slowly slid their way down. They were always antsy to move, but all three dogs would sit side by side in the *stay* position and wait for my command. I would wait until the children were down and had moved out of the way to signal to the dogs that they were free to move. The command was *Go free!* I would say this to them with excitement and conviction and they would bark and jump and run down the stairs so fast that I had to be sure the babies were out of the pathway of the wildness that was galloping down the stairs to head straight to the back door and out into the yard, where they would jump all over each other and run around as if they had never been outside before. Day after day, the excitement of the first morning run to the backyard was as if it was their very first time doing it. Each new day was filled with excitement and doggy joy!

The dog sitting at the top of the stairs, looking down and so ready to make a move toward the back door to go run and play outside—that is how I had been feeling for years. I waited and waited not nearly as patiently as my dogs did for that signal to finally go free. I know what it feels like to want something different but have no idea how to make it happen. I also know what it feels like when the opportunity tells you that it's time to go free and you finally do it. As I explained earlier in the book, I also know what it feels like to think I'm finally free in a new place only to be perilously let down because I landed in what can only be described as the wrong place.

The dogs, when they went free from the stairs to the yard, had a direct path that they would follow. They knew exactly where they were going and what lay ahead of that exact pathway. Having a clear direction changes things significantly. I know the difference on a deeply soulful level of what that experience feels like both in alignment and out. I still trust that everything happens for a specific reason and that divine timing is paramount. I know that the wrong place for me was still a very important stop along the way to my arrival at the place that feeds my soul so deeply and richly. I'm thankful I only had to stay in that spot for one year before making my permanent residence in what I call heaven on earth. It was an important stop for my personal growth, but I am incredibly grateful I didn't get stuck in it.

Not every move we make will lead us to the paradise we seek. That doesn't mean you stop trying or that you stop trusting the process. Trust that we are all being divinely guided all the days of our lives. I know what it feels like to finally get out of the box that was always too small and allow myself to soar and go free. I know it so well that I recognize that same pent-up energy in other people and I want more than anything for all of us to live the life we might only be starting to imagine. Give yourself permission to dream and explore within yourself the life you want to live. Open yourself up to the possibilities and magic that life has to offer.

Should you choose to begin making plans to take the steps into something new, trust that the seeds you sow will bloom. Eventually the seed will sprout and it will take you through the entire growing and blooming season into a life that genuinely honors who you are and feeds you from the deepest, most beloved and hidden parts of your soul. All will find the light if you allow yourself to see it and trust the pathway toward it.

Count Your Blessings and Return Them

There is always a place in life to give back, to show gratitude differently than only cultivating an internal practice of gratitude. For example, several countries in the Mediterranean feed and honor stray cats. They have feeding programs to make sure the cats never go hungry. Everywhere you look, there are cat bowls of food and water in front of all kinds of homes. Parks are filled with cat houses for them to sleep in. People here take care of the animals and they take care of the people.

Anywhere you look on these islands, you can watch human acts of kindness. Blessed are those that know the goodness when it comes. The last time I visited Malta's sister island of Gozo, I was amazed to find cat feeding and drinking vending machines in certain populated areas. There were holes in which to empty your water bottles that put water into the bowl and another bowl at the bottom filled with food. You also can put coins in to help pay for the food and water. Greece is another country that is a well known for taking care of its stray cats in much the same way. It is a fond memory of many travelers who visit these islands to watch the kindness in action to those who cannot do for themselves.

I love to watch the cats come out of their hiding spots to go eat a meal. Even when I come with cans of wet food (which I keep in my car and in my purse to have on hand), I always find bowls of both dry food and water already sitting out for them. The cat feeding programs are organized through volunteers in each town and the food is paid for by the local council. They sit on people's doorsteps, at every park, near all the cat houses that are under public benches and other areas. There is a public park in every town on both islands, and the towns themselves are very tiny, so you find parks everywhere. In each park, you will find cat houses stacked in rows and feeding areas. On the main island, there is an actual cat park that is easy to spot because of the enormous cat statue that looks a lot like Pete the Cat from the children's storybooks. That is the biggest cat park on the island, and cats that roam the streets by day make their way there by night to sleep.

People here do not see the stray cats as nuisances, but as beloved friends that we all support and feed. They are not gathered up and put into shelters only to be put down two days later for space. Cats are allowed to live free here on the island, and we all do our part. There are no-kill animal shelters that house cats and dogs and offer them for adoption, along with feral cat catch-and-release programs to spay and neuter and return them where they found them. In any tourist shop, you can purchase a calendar titled *Cats of Malta* to help support these programs.

If you are wondering how you can be of service, I have some ideas. The top two ways to give are with your time or money. It doesn't have to be either-or, but those are the two most precious offerings you can give to anyone who can't do for themselves. You can make a financial donation to any group or practice that helps the world in some way or you can donate your time by helping network or showing up and providing hands-on help.

I drop everything if there is an animal in need near me. It's not something I go looking for, but if I happen across a sick or lost animal, I am the one to scoop it up and go to the vet or take it in and do what I can to help it. I will always try to find the owner or figure out a plan B for them. That is my time and I donate it when I can. I will cancel whatever is on the agenda if I see an animal in desperate need in front of me. I also donate money where I can. Children's services, animal rescues, and any other organization you can think of all depend heavily on donations. I still help to network animal rescue groups and animals in the shelters back in the US through social media.

You do whatever you are able to do without overtaxing yourself. Giving back will take you out of a more self-centered place and put something cleaner and purer into your heart and mind. If you wonder what you can do or if it's even worth it if you can't offer much, trust that anything is better than nothing and do what you can. I keep a good stock of canned cat food in my trunk. Whenever I see a stray cat, I feed them. It's a little thing that might not seem like much, but to that cat, I might be the reason they were fed that day. And hopefully the next day someone else is the reason they eat again and again. Human kindness can build on itself into something magnificent. Be part of that growing.

Kindness Carries

I have noticed that there is a sort of understanding that the local cats seem to have. They know how to fit into the world around them. You can find cats outside many restaurants, and if you put your hand down to signal to them that you will drop some food for them, they will come to you quickly and stand by your lowered hand. However, you don't find the cats walking on the tables or doing obnoxious things to try to get the food (the way my spoiled cat does at home!). I've even seen cats outside in the city gathering areas where tons of people bring their dogs to dine, each unfazed by the other. Add to that the pigeons that walk freely in between and all around the tables and not one of them chases the other! It's like the animals here are taught to get along and do right by each other, and that's how they will continue to be invited the next time. Somehow these animals all seem to understand the rules of social graces.

Kindness carries out into the world around us. It begins small and grows out of itself. Kindness, compassion, and gratitude are practiced in spades on these islands. Kindness prevails here, although not so much when people are driving (which is madness). Maybe living near water softens us somehow. It calms us and reminds us that the world is so much bigger than our problems. Maybe people aren't as angry because there is so much open nature nearby to bring you back to the center more quickly. Whatever it is, I will take it happily and be thankful.

On several streets on the island, you will find large donation boxes for people here: one for clothes, one for shoes, and one for books or toys. There is always a place where you can donate. You can also call the local nuns and they will show up in their vans to pick up food to give to the children. I believe now more than ever, upon witnessing it in action, that when communities come together to help one another, everyone in the surrounding area benefits enormously. The animals are no exception here. How someone treats animals and children tells me everything I need to know about them. Here, both are treated with a great deal of love, respect, and reverence.

Ta' Pinu Church of Miracles

There are a lot of practices that people in this culture do to make sure they never take God's blessings for granted. Whether this is with a good harvest for the year, new family members, or improved health, it is important to always count your blessings and give back.

There is a large church on the smaller sister island of Gozo called the Ta' Pinu National Shrine. It is known as the "Church of Miracles" and is considered to be the most famous church in Gozo, attracting people from all over the world. There is a lot of history to this once-small chapel. Originally known as Tal-Gentili and dedicated to the Assumption of the Blessed Mother, the small chapel was built before 1845 CE.[29] In 1575 Pope Gregory XIII sent a man to assess the chapel, and that man determined that the church was not worth keeping and ordered it to be demolished. When the demolition began, one of the workmen broke his arm upon the first strike. This was the moment when everyone realized that this church was not to be destroyed and instead preserved.

In 1598 the church property changed hands and the name was changed to Ta' Pinu, named after the church procurator, Pinu Gauci. It was he who commissioned a painting of the Assumption of Our Lady, which remains untouched on the altar to this day. The huge sanctuary that one can see today was not fully built until 1920. The old chapel now stands behind the large neo-Romanesque shrine. You would not recognize it as the small chapel, because they built the two churches into each other seamlessly. That small original chapel still houses the painting of the Assumption of Our Lady, and you can find it in the back of the church behind the main altar.

Locals believe the painting of the Assumption of Our Lady to be a miracle in and of itself. The story goes that a local woman named Karmni Grima from the town of Gharb heard a voice calling to her from inside the chapel in 1883. She heard the voice call out to her three times: "Come! Come! Come!" The location of Ta' Pinu even today would be considered

---

29. Fava, "The Miraculous Story of Our Lady of Ta' Pinu National Shrine, in Gozo."

out in the middle of nowhere. The drive to get there is not a little one. At that time, it was out in the middle of deserted fields.

When Karmni heard the voice call to her, she looked around and knew that it could not be an actual person calling to her, as there was no one within miles. So she kept walking. Then she heard the voice say again, "Come, come, today, because a year will have passed before you will be able to visit this place again."[30] With that, she approached the chapel and peeked in the small window but saw no one. She went inside and decided to pray. As she was sitting there, she felt an experience of "ineffable rapture" and was told by that same voice, "Recite three Hail Marys in remembrance of the three days during which my body lay in the tomb." She did as she was told.

There is a book documenting this story written by Mgr. Nicholas J. Cauchi, Bishop of Gozo from 1972 to 2005. In the book, he says that while the woman kept this to herself for more than two years, she did finally share her story with Frangisk Portelli, a man who was well known for his devotion to Our Lady of Ta' Pinu. His heart filled with gladness as she shared this with him. It turned out that he too had heard voices from the shrine that asked him to say prayers in honor of Christ's hidden shoulder wound, which was inflicted when he was carrying the cross. Portelli reported that his mother had been healed miraculously by the Blessed Virgin of Ta' Pinu. The story of both of these local people being spoken to spread quickly throughout the town. It has also been documented that Karmni's home was visited by the Blessed Virgin of Ta' Pinu. Today, her home remains open to visitors. Also to this day, you will find above the basilica's main door a mosaic of Madonna and Child with the words "Ejja!Ejja! Ejja!" which in Maltese means "Come! Come! Come!"[31]

In front of the shrine is a hill known by the locals as Ta' Ghammar Hill.[32] As you make your way to the top, you will find fourteen statues made of marble that represent the Stations of the Cross. When you walk

---

30. Fava, "The Miraculous Story of Our Lady of Ta' Pinu National Shrine, in Gozo."

31. Fava, "The Miraculous Story of Our Lady of Ta' Pinu National Shrine, in Gozo."

32. A Wandering Medic, "Ta' Pinu National Shrine: An Architectural Masterpiece."

inside, two large white marble angels sit cross-legged holding big bowls of holy water on each side of the entrance. That was my favorite thing to see the first time I walked inside, not knowing anything of the lore of this church or the secret side rooms that store the thanksgivings from the miracles people received after their first visit.

People come from all over the world to pray for healing at the "Church of Miracles." Many people also return to Ta' Pinu to give their testimony of the miracles that occurred following their first visit and prayers for the intercession of the Blessed Mother. There are two rooms on each side of the alter that are filled with relics that reflect the miracles that God has bestowed upon them. There are walking canes on the wall where people learned to walk again. There are back braces, leg casts, and many framed baby bonnets and booties with pictures of babies that were finally conceived after a pilgrimage to this church. This beautiful and enormous church is a site for people to make their way to look for miracles. And many times, and for many people, they find them.

Hal-Saflieni Hypogeum

It's not just churches in Malta that offer miracles that people travel from all over the world to experience. When I said I was moving to Malta, I was surprised at how many people sent me information about the Hypogeum, the famous Oracle Sound Chamber. This chamber is one of the world's oldest preserved sites, and it stores many stories within its walls. This includes a temple, a cemetery, and a funeral hall.

Evidence suggests that it was in 4000 BCE that the people from Malta and Gozo built places to ritualize death. The Hypogeum that still stands underground was one of the first to be built to house the bodies and support the ritual of the dead. It is believed that there are over six thousand bodies buried within its walls. The entire thing sits underground and was not discovered until the early 1900s when construction workers were digging for a well for a house and discovered three underground levels to this enclosure!

According to a 2017 Smithsonian article, the upper level of the Hypogeum is the oldest and is the passageway to the burial chambers carved from caves.[33] Archaeologists believe that the funeral processions originate within the chamber. You can find one of the original graves intact there. The middle level is where the rituals were believed to have taken place. This is where the oracle room is located. This is a room that visitors can walk through, and it is in this "sound healing oracle room" that the sound waves are said to kill cancer cells within the human body. This is due to the healing properties within the stone surrounding the area.

Within the stone walls, the frequency is 111 hertz, a number that is extremely important in the world of complementary medicine. It is believed that this sound frequency offered inside the chamber (the Oracle Sound Chamber, to be more specific) along with what is known as a "divine frequency principle" meet together in the same space within the sound chamber. This sound frequency is believed to be a direct line to the gods and can offer a trance state for deep cellular healing to occur. According to the research, "MRI scans show that the brain switches off the prefrontal cortex and deactivates the language center that is responsible for holistic processing, creativity, intuition, and inducing a phase at exactly 111 Hz. This reaction results in a divine level of meditation, the trance that some believe allows you to get connected with the universe, God or a creator."[34]

When I moved here, I could not wait to go and visit this Oracle Sound Chamber. I wanted to sit inside the oracle room and see if I could feel the energy of the healing vibrations. No such luck. It's a guided tour and you have no time to sit down anywhere. You put on headphones and listen to the stories of the history and only see the actual oracle chamber circle. You do not get to go sit inside it. I can tell you this though: it feels overwhelming in there. It's sensory overload, especially for a sensitive person such as myself. There are folk tales and scary tales that have occurred

33. McKenna, "Malta's Hypogeum, One of the World's Best Preserved Prehistoric Sites, Reopens to the Public."
34. Interesting Engineering. "Mysterious Ancient Temples Resonate at the 'Holy Frequency.'"

inside the Hypogeum. It's a lot to take in. But if I were planning a visit and hoping for miracles and healing and I wanted to do the pilgrimage to the church of Ta' Pinu in Gozo for miracles, I would highly recommend visiting Malta's Hypogeum Sound Oracle Chamber whether you believe in the healing sounds or not, just to double up on your chances for miracles to bless your way. It was certainly high on my list of must-sees when I arrived here. I am grateful for the chance to be inside this place.

People travel around the world in search of healing waters, healthy air, dietary secrets, and really anything for a healthier and more vibrant life. People travel to the Mediterranean to learn the diets and culture that support the healthiest way of life in the world. But it's more than following a Mediterranean diet. It's more than just visiting the sea. It's diving into a culture that still believes in the magic and power of healing and miracles and is not closed off to the possibilities of where those can be found. For example, there are no poisonous snakes on the island, because when St. Paul the Apostle (who discovered Malta) was bitten by a snake, he sucked the poison out of it and no snake here carries poison to this day. It is still considered a gift from St. Paul. People here don't scoff and laugh at this description. They believe it with absolute conviction.

There is still magic in the world. There always has been. It isn't lost in a place like this. Stories and history and a deep sense of wonder are still passed down through the generations here. St. Patrick is the saint who rid the snakes of poison in Ireland. There are lots of stories of saints and angels doing something spectacular that either people fully believe or write off as folklore. But even those who claim not to have a superstitious bone in their body might be the athlete who doesn't wash his socks for the entire season or only wears certain clothes when watching a sports team, or someone like me who only picks up a penny for good luck if it's on heads. We all have some sort of belief in something a little bit more magical, don't we? Life would be a lot duller if we didn't have our own special something to believe in.

The Lady of the Grotto Who Cried Tears of Blood

It wasn't until I was doing research for this book that I was first introduced to the miracle that sits with the Lady of the Grotto. The story goes like this. The Virgin Mary appeared first to a hunter in a cave in the year 1400 CE. Not long after this occurred, the site was turned into a chapel, then a large church and a priory. To honor the visit of the Virgin Mary, they have a large statue of Mary holding the baby Jesus at the bottom of the cave where the hunter first saw her appear. There are too many stories of miracles to list that occurred within this cave with the Lady of the Grotto.

The statue of the Divine Mother holding her baby stands at the bottom of a staircase into a cave. In 1981 they brought in a replica of the statue from Italy due to the damage to the original statue. This statue is guarded behind glass and wrought iron lattice, so you cannot touch it. She stands in water and the cave is lit up by candles that burn around the entire area. Rosaries hang from every place on which something can be hung. It is magnificent and highly auspicious. As you walk down the steps into the dark cave, the floor is inundated with lit candles in red jars all around her. When I looked at the statue, it felt as if she was looking back at me. There are a few rows of pews for people to kneel on and pray for her intercession. In 1999 she was found to cry tears of human blood, and this has been witnessed twice since.[35]

Malta is not the only place that has a statue of the Virgin Mary who has cried tears of blood. This has also occurred in Australia, Ireland, and Italy.[36] Because this story made me so curious, I went to see her for myself. I sat down in front of her and prayed for something very specific for my healing. The following day, it was granted. While one person would chalk this up to coincidence, someone like me could never discount the prayer that was answered. This island is full of magic and mystery and history and faith, and I feel it and delight in diving into it. I believe that the more you open yourself up to receiving miracles, the more often they will come to you. The Lady of the Grotto most certainly did not disappoint.

35. Fava, "The Miraculous Story of the Maltese Lady of the Grotto."
36. Drury, "Tears of Blood! Here Are Some of Malta's Most Famous 'Miracles.'"

It is like a breath of fresh air to my belief system to be among people with such a deep and rich faith in so many things. Never underestimate that there are secrets and divine treasures scattered and hidden all over the world for you to find and uncover if that is something you are called to do. The earth is an enormous place. There are so many incredible things to do and see. There are also so many ways to be the giver, the believer, the faithful, the supporter, and the light to those who are not yet able to find it on their own.

Food for Thought: Simple Questions with Deeper Answers

It is always wise to stop and ask ourselves questions to get clear on our thoughts and feelings about a particular subject. Here are a few simple questions that might elicit more thought-provoking answers:

- What are you thankful for?
- Who are you thankful for?
- What practices do you engage in to calm, center, balance, and connect yourself with your higher self?
- What are some of the ways that you are leaving the world better than the way you found it?

Food Tip and Recipe

My vivacious and beautiful friend Michelle makes traditional coconut balls as her special gift to all her friends and family. I know that on my birthday I can hope get a container of perfectly round and wonderfully delicious coconut balls from her. It's something that my children and I all look forward to whenever a special occasion comes around. Since being here, I have noticed that those coconut balls, along with many variations, seem to be one of the main staples for simple, not too heavy desserts all over the island. Even my children were taught how to make them in school this year because they are so common and easy to make. These little dessert bites are small enough that you can have just one or two without guilt or overfilling yourself after a meal.

I was in a café recently and took note of all the different balls they had. They all looked so beautiful stacked so perfectly on every tray side by side. Here is a list of the different dessert balls for sale that afternoon to give you an idea of what I mean:

Traditional coconut balls
Limoncello balls
Almond truffle
Torrone (with a powdered sugar coating)
Bordeaux (with a dark chocolate cocoa powder coating)
Caffe (a coffee mixed covering)
Caramel and hazelnut
Pistachio praline
Cacao and orange
Maraschino (with white chocolate and cherry)
Forest fruit

Traditional Coconut Balls
(Recipe by Michelle Abela)

INGREDIENTS

1 package tea biscuits (Here we use a brand name of coffee biscuits. In the US you could use graham crackers.)
½ cup (50 grams) shredded coconut
1 can sweetened condensed milk
⅓ cup (35 grams) cocoa powder
Optional: a touch of whiskey or bourbon
Coconut shavings, cocoa powder, or other outside coating

DIRECTIONS

Crush a sleeve of the biscuits finely. Add the coconut, sweetened condensed milk, and cocoa powder. Mix the ingredients until it forms one big ball. From there, make smaller balls to your liking and then roll them in coconut shavings or cocoa powder or whatever you choose for the outside. Let sit for a few hours in the refrigerator and serve.

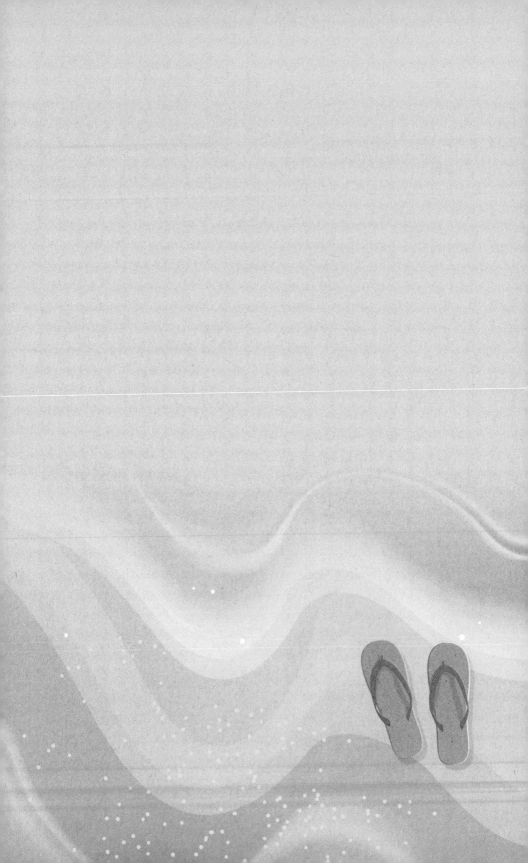

Chapter 10
Celebrate Everything

The Mediterranean people know how to party. They work hard when they need to and they play hard when it's time to. What I love most is that they celebrate everything. Guilty pleasures are not guilty here. They are simply pleasures. Pleasure is not something negative or taboo. Fireworks, parades, feast days, wine, bread, olive oils, and simple foods are found everywhere here. People here don't work long days. They cut out in the middle and go for a walk or a swim in the sea before either returning to work or deciding that this day should be shorter. The people of the Mediterranean celebrate life! The world here is not led by guilt, but by celebration. They relish seeing people happy, eating, drinking, and playing. What more to life is there than this?

What Does It Mean to Celebrate Everything?

Let's start at the center and work our way out with this one. Begin by focusing on the most precious connection to life that we often overlook or take for granted. It's our breath. Your breath is the beginning piece to acknowledging and celebrating your life's very existence. Breathe slowly in and out and feel your lungs and belly expand as you do so. Your breath tells exactly what your mental state is in every single moment. It is the most present-tense indicator of your quality of life at any given time. If you want to know where you are within your state of mental and emotional health, you need to do nothing more than check your breath and listen in. The calmer and more present you are, the more silent your breath will be. It will be full in both the inhale and the exhale but without you needing to put any power behind it. It's not so much a long inhale or exhale, but more that it feels like a complete inhale or exhale.

Your breath leads the way for you. It will accept all the oxygen that it needs in any single breath and it will release the carbon dioxide back into the world. It doesn't require any thought. It is simply a flow of health that feels peaceful, fulfilled, and satisfied. This kind of breathing doesn't happen all that often, to be honest, unless you are thoughtful about your breathing practices and aware of the connection between your breathing and your emotions. It occurs when you are in your most pure and peaceful state of mind. For some, this happens only in deep sleep. For others, it becomes a daily practice that is noticed and appreciated throughout each day.

If you are not currently at your most peaceful and comfortable state within, the breath can become more erratic, more shallow, less frequent, and without a steady flow, depending on how you are feeling in the moment. Anxious breaths tend to be short and shallow and linger up at the top of your chest and collarbones. Angry breaths tend to be both loud and held and only come and go in short spurts to keep you from passing out. Sad breaths feel long, but you never seem to get a full breath even though the length of time for any given breath seems like it should give way to a complete feeling of breathing. Scared breathing almost stops completely. Short and high are the scary breaths. Excited breaths are much the same, since the same hormones are releasing and coursing through our bodies during either of these two feelings.

Where are you in this moment as you read through this? Is your breath soft, silent, long, and fulfilled? Or is it loud, short, or uneven? Begin with becoming aware of the sound of your breathing and then allow it to calm as your awareness gives it a little extra support through the acknowledgment. Once you feel your breath slowing and steadying, give thanks to yourself and your efforts for making your body feel like a more comfortable home for your soul to dwell in. That's the first way to begin celebrating everything. This is also where practices such as prayer, meditation, centering, contemplation, and gratitude mindsets can begin to shape the breath and the thoughts into a more substantial whole. Without having to regulate either your thoughts or your breath, they simultaneously regulate and merge into each other. Then with ease, the mind and body merge into a single-pointed focus toward something more sacred and healthier.

As we get further into celebrating everything, we take it out of the inner circle of body-mind and begin to notice ourselves and our thoughts according to external stimuli. You are the only person in the whole world who knows just how difficult some things are for you to do, so you are the only person who can congratulate yourself when you do them. For example, when I was going through my younger years of terrible anxiety, panic, and agoraphobia, I had a huge fear of going to the grocery store. I can't explain why exactly. It was just a trigger spot for me. Only I know how big of a deal it was when I would get through a full shopping trip without skipping items just to get out faster. Only I knew the effort it took for me to slow myself down and try to center my thoughts and ground my body while standing in the middle of any given aisle so that I could continue to shop.

Only I knew that I could talk myself down from the edges of hysteria and rearrange my thought patterns to recognize that even though I was afraid, I was also attached to that fear as some sort of bizarre cycle I was stuck in. It was as if it was as much a play practice as it was a practice to overcome my scary thoughts. For a long time, I liked having my scary thoughts to contend with. It left me out of the rest of the world. I never would have admitted to that fact back then, but there is always some kind of reward in engaging with the scary thoughts until you finally learn to master the strength of your mind to overcome them. Sometimes we create scary thoughts to consume our minds so that we can disengage from everything else in the outside world.

I had to learn to give myself big praise when I would finally make it out of the store with my shopping bags in hand. To someone else, this would have sounded ridiculous. The whole thing would have sounded so meaningless to give myself props for making it safely out of a grocery store. It wasn't for anyone else though. It was my own issue, and so it was from myself where the thanks and praise had to originate. With every single trip to the grocery store and with every little self-congratulation I extended, I began to celebrate my efforts instead of using negative dialogue to put myself down. That is a celebration!

To celebrate everything means to celebrate all of the tiny nuances that you face in your daily life and give thanks for the way that you handled them. Celebrating yourself starts in the smallest ways and then grows into bigger platforms as you go. Always come back to the center when you need to. Come back to your breath and work your way out from there. Everything you do that makes you feel glad for having done it, give yourself quick praises and little pats on the back. Start simple and then do more things that make you feel celebrated. Then take that same behavior and turn it around and take it to things outside of yourself to acknowledge and be glad for.

Be supportive of your friends and neighbors and help wherever you can. Those small, seemingly insignificant things you had to overcome within yourself also exist in some form or fashion for every single person around you. No one is nearly as together as you imagine them to be. Start to emanate the kindness that you are now practicing for yourself and turn that inside out and offer it for your friends and family. When you create a voice of awareness, love, acceptance, and gratitude inside yourself, you can easily become that voice for other people. It doesn't work the other way around though, if you focus on the outside before doing the work from deep inside. It is truly an inside job. That's the difference between living authentically and living only skin deep. This, for me, is where celebrating everything originates. You celebrate every single little thing that lives within you and around you that elevates your state of being. Start small and go big. Give yourself and everyone around you permission to celebrate life!

Celebrate the Harvest

On the day that I went to the potato farm to meet with Paul, the potato farmer, there were several tables set up outside left over from the evening before. Near the tables on the outskirts of the potato fields sits a wood oven made of stone. He said that on the final day of the harvest, the entire family comes to pick their potato and cook them in that oven. The kids, the grandkids, the cousins, the nieces and nephews—all of them come to join the family party to celebrate a great harvest. He said they all pick their potato and put it into the oven along with the meat. Then they put fresh bread on all the tables and use their own olive oil also grown on their farm. They have bottles of wine (for which they grow the grapes) and drink into the wee hours of the morning in celebration.

I arrived just after their celebration, and Paul had to take me to a second potato field to show me potatoes that were still in the ground, because the ones at his farm on the first property had all just been harvested. That is how I was able to see the tables and chairs still left out from the celebration the night before. In Malta, due to the small amount of land space and also wind issues, many farmers have several different areas in which they grow their crops. Paul took me to his second location, where they had not yet completed the harvest, so I could dig the potatoes out of the dirt myself. This also means that their big celebration doesn't only happen once all the farms are finished. They gather and celebrate after each field has been emptied!

This culture doesn't ask that you wait to celebrate until the very last potato on the very last field has been harvested. It asks that with each field and harvest, you come together with your family and honor that you had a great crop! Then you do it again with the next and the next. Parties and family gatherings with wine, bread, fresh cheese, and fresh oil aren't something you save up to do. It's something you do any time there is something to celebrate! You can always find a reason to gather friends and family and celebrate something here! Gratitude is an energy that grows from itself. Offer thanks and praise every chance you are given and watch how it grows.

When I visited an olive oil farmer, he had the same sort of setup at his place. Rows of long tables were set out and a wood stove was just nearby. He said that they too celebrate at the end of the season, and they also gather and celebrate with every group that travels to Malta to study with him. He said he teaches the students to taste the different olive oils and then makes the traditional Maltese ftira sandwich finished off with their favorite olive oil to celebrate the end of their visit. They celebrate a good harvest in hopes that more will come.

Celebrations of giving thanks are huge here. It is not gluttonous; it does not cost a fortune. It's coming together to celebrate family and friends and to acknowledge the blessings that have been bestowed upon them. Celebration is an important part of the growing and farming lifestyle. It is also an important element in their community's way of life that this part of the world continues to foster. They celebrate as an act of giving thanks to their creator for blessing them with a bountiful harvest.

The Village Feasts

Do you remember the time in your growing up when practically every week was spent gathering to watch a big parade, followed by a wild celebration with big bands, throwing confetti, and seeing giant fireworks displays? No? Just once in the summer and once on New Year's Eve? That is what it's like here every week, especially in summer when it's warm and sunny and beautiful. There are sixty village feasts a year in Malta and twenty celebrated in Gozo,[37] and those are just the village feasts! That doesn't count the other larger celebrations such as Karnival, where the island blows up with elaborate costumes, parades, and parties day into night into more days for a week (which inspired the New Orleans version of Mardi Gras).

If you want to find a local celebration here, you don't have to look far to find one. The people from all around gather to celebrate and play together. Community is everything to the locals here. And the food is the

37. Visit Malta, "Village Festas."

glue that keeps this beautiful community celebrating together. Everyone is invited. There is no special Evite sent only to a chosen few. Instead, it's your elderly neighbor, the family from across the street, your friends at school, your friends at church, your friends from your sports teams, your teachers, your principal, your grocery worker—everyone you have ever seen and people you've never seen all gathering together week by week to play together, to sing and dance. Wine, oil, and bread sit on practically every table at every feast.

The village feasts are put on by each local parish, and the church is decorated with hundreds of light bulbs up and down the front of the church. Since there are many palm trees in front of these magnificent churches, they wrap lights all around the palm trees in honor of the holidays and festivals. Each town is represented by a different saint, and in each of those towns they celebrate with parades and gatherings for a feast. The *festa* is made up of a procession of the village's patron saint, followed by fireworks, bands, and exciting celebrations throughout the town. Almost daily you can hear the fireworks being set off. The children grow up to celebrate life often and in a multitude of ways, and they celebrate together as a community, not just with their own families but all together in the towns themselves. It's a public celebration for all to come and join.

I have to believe that this is what sets the foundation for a much more inclusive culture than I have ever been privy to before. It is a culture passed along through the generations that there is always time to set aside to celebrate and worship in a way that is not so daunting but instead is an actual celebration of life—quite a wild celebration of life beyond anything I've ever seen before! Over here, it is a way of life and nothing at all to feel guilty about. This is life! Celebrations abound to acknowledge the living and honor the dead. There are ceremonies all around the world that practice such things. We could learn so much from those who celebrate life so vigorously.

It's Time to Dive In!

I get a lot of my information and insight about Malta from David, the man who maintains our pool. I love him. I follow him outside almost every time he's here to ask any number of random questions in learning the ropes to establish my new life here. He used to be a pizza maker. He too has a wood oven at his house and makes individual pizzas for everyone in the family when they come together to celebrate anything. He never hesitates to share with me anything I want to know, such as "the coarsest winds come from the south," as he often says. I understand this more now as my car and the ground are covered in brown sand from the Sahara Desert. It makes me feel like I'm swallowing chalk. What was covered in yellow (pollen) back in Georgia and caused everyone to have severe allergies has now turned brown here in Malta when the winds come in from the desert in Africa.

David also explained to me that the winds from the north come from Sicily. I once asked him when the swimming season was going to be starting again. Someone told me we get nine months of summer and three months of cold, and I have since decided that whoever that was could not have been a local, because it is not true. It was my first winter in Malta and I was trying to gauge when it would finally be warm enough again to use the pool. David told me that there is an actual date that marks when the swimming season begins again. It follows one of the great feast day celebrations, the Feast of St. Gregory, the patron saint of musicians, singers, students, and teachers. This feast celebration doesn't just go through one local town but through almost the entire southern portion of the island, from a town centrally located named Żejtun to the southern edge of the island at the fishing village of Marsaxlokk. People who are involved in the procession take turns holding the statue of St. Gregory as they walk through their town until they all finally land at the end of the island and at the edge of the water.[38]

---

38. Malta.com. "Feast of St. Gregory in Zejtun."

The Feast of St. Gregory is always on the first Wednesday after Easter Sunday. They are not strictly weekend celebrators here in Malta! The feast day falls on the saint's official day of celebration no matter what day of the week it is. Once the parade has gone through the towns and everyone arrives in the fishing village at the water, people celebrate big by drinking wine and eating fresh bread with olive oil and dancing and singing until enough wine has been consumed that the first crazy, brave soul strips down to their little tiny skivvies and dives into the sea!

From there, one by one and then in a crowd, the most daring men, women, and children strip down to their bathing suits and dive right in. The sea is warmer than the swimming pools far longer into the cold season, but it is still very cold, and the feast day occurs when it's not yet nearly warm enough to enjoy a sea swim but you have had enough wine to make it work. What a lovely way to grow up! What an amazing introduction to the concept that life is meant to be played with and celebrated! Ah, to be foolish and daring enough to risk getting too cold in your attempt to take that dive into the sea!

What if we were to take a page from this culture and choose to dive into our own life just a little bit more daringly? What if we lifted some of the parameters that we have set for ourselves and offered ourselves and our neighbors a little less judgment and a lot more grace? Wouldn't you be able to breathe just a little bit more deeply? What if we let go of the reins and only worried about our own home but still were fully present to the idea that we can worry about ourselves and still come together for our communities? We help ourselves by helping others, but not with so many ridiculous rules that so many of us have come up with.

So much judgment and so many political divisions blind us to the truth that community is not for only one group to be included in. Helping others or becoming a part of a community does not require you to change yourself into anything you don't want to become. It asks you to be of service where you can without drowning yourself to help anyone else. Maybe we celebrate today by having some wine or grape juice with fresh bread and high-quality extra virgin olive oil? Even that, something so small, can make you feel like you are entering into a different space within yourself.

Whatever it is that feeds your soul in a richer and more meaningful way, it's time to dive into exactly that! It's time to breathe a little more consciously, to think a little less rigidly, to show up for community events or gatherings more, and to stop trying so hard to get anyone to believe or behave however you think it should be done. Enjoy living a little bit more and judging a whole lot less. This is what I love the most about living here. No one is ever trying to make me believe something or join something or push an agenda on me. They just want to come together to support and celebrate. If you don't want to bother with deep discussions or share anything about financial, political, medical, or other sensitive topics, then you don't have to! No one is overly concerned with those aspects of a person. And when you come to play, no one wants to hear about that stuff anyway. *Are you good people?* That is all we need to know. The rest will sort itself out.

Working with Nature

I've met some people here who I would consider to be the hardest workers I have ever seen in my life, and for that, my perception of life has changed. It has become closer to the earth. Seeing how food is grown, tended to, and harvested has been incredibly insightful. It makes me realize all the more that everything matters. Everything counts. You must pair up with Mother Nature or she will destroy your family dynasty, and they know it. The people who work close to the earth understand this basic truth and live accordingly. Their entire survival depends on the timing of the seeds to the blooms of every flower, plant, vegetable, and fruit that grows. They aren't doing it just for themselves. They are doing it to continue their family's legacy. They are doing it because it's the only thing they have ever known to do.

My dear friend Natasha in the fishing village told me she has never had a job a day in her life. She says she doesn't go to work—she helps her family. She doesn't consider it something she has to do, but instead something she is called to do. To her, it is an honor to help her father and brother and nieces and nephews. She strives daily to honor her late mother. Anyone who meets her for even five minutes will learn that there is nothing more important in the world to her than her family. Her family, by the way, is not just her blood relatives. Her family is all the fishermen in the village. It's the servers in the cafés. It's me. It's you. She once caught a child and saved him just before he fell into the sea when his parents were not looking. She takes so much pride in simply being a good person—actually, in being the best person she can be. She sets up cat houses in her village and feeds the cats every day. She takes pots of hot coffee out to all the fishermen in the various boats lined up, not just to her father. That way they don't have to get off the boat and go buy coffee. She brings trays of coffee and cups from her own home to make sure they all have something to drink.

Natasha makes me want to be a better person every time I'm near her. She reminds me that life doesn't have to be so fast or so complicated and doesn't have to always be so hard. Life is a gift, and she doesn't miss an opportunity to give thanks and give back to her village. She is like a little angel of the fishing village, and everyone cherishes her and her incredibly peaceful heart. She also drinks beer for breakfast. This woman absolutely fascinates me and makes me giggle all the time I'm near her! She sits at the table with me to meet for a coffee and instead simply points her finger at the table when the local server says, "The water of life, right?" And that means Cisk (sounds like "Chisk"), the local Maltese beer. That is their water of life!

People I've met all around the island who fish or farm are so pure of heart and so uniquely delightful to my soul. They are doing their life's work through the foods they grow; it is their love offering to every person who comes to buy it and take it home with them to feed their families. They know that the people who buy their food trust them and count on them. The people on the whole island, especially the farmers and fishermen in each area, pray for one another and help each other in ways that you only hear about in stories. The simple concept of *love thy neighbor* still exists as an action here.

Nature has never been so close up and personal to me as it is now. I see the farmers who work practically from dusk to dawn and then begin again in the wee hours of the early morning or late night. I see the fisherman like Natasha's father who leaves at 3:30 a.m. every morning to go out to sea and bring the fish back for their families to sell. Their timing depends on the waves of the sea and what fish are migrating at that time. These aren't stories of the olden days when people still went out and caught their food. This is daily life here on this small island, with a heartbeat so strong that you can feel its pulse beneath your every move if you silence yourself and listen long enough. This is calling up George, a cheese maker in Gozo, and telling him I want to bring my family over to visit and he gets up extra early to make us some fresh ġbejniet so I can take it home with me. He brings my girls in to meet all the sheep and goats and asks us if there is anything else we want to see before we go. This is a man who has been making cheese for over seventy years since he was sitting in his mother's kitchen at ten years old learning how.

These friends whom I have been blessed to find are utterly exquisite. I wish I could truly express the love and adoration I have for every single one of these most deliciously sweet people! They are so much love! I can feel it, I can taste it, and I can reciprocate the best way I know how, which is to honor them all as I introduce them to the rest of the world as the most beautiful expression of human kindness, compassion, hard work, dedication, and love that I have ever been fortunate enough to witness. They learned from their mothers and fathers and their grandmothers and grandfathers and the party continues.

When I first meet any farmer or fisherman, it's to do a live video interview, so it's mostly business. Then, when the magazine comes out, I bring my family back to their farm and hand-deliver each print magazine. That way my family gets to see what I've been up to and what I've gotten to see at the different places. For example, Tony, a prickly pear farmer I interviewed, grows a ton of fruits for his jams on a property filled with old caves from the days when the cavaliers would bring their prisoners. He brought his dog and I brought my husband and kids to hike all the way up inside those caves. Tony has a sense of humor that would make anyone blush. You almost have to brace yourself for whatever might come out of his mouth, but I love it. He cracks me up. We call and check in with each other quite often.

That's what people do here. They maintain their friendships with such passion and consistency that I am still learning not to let too much time pass before meeting up again. There is a "once you're friends, you're family" mentality here that I'm still getting used to. On the day we did the salt interview with Josephine and her family, as soon as we left, she messaged me saying, "Okay, now you are family. Anything you ever need, just ask." When I go to Gozo, I always make time to visit her at the shop and she always has cookies ready for my girls. That is the way of the world here. It has asked me to be a much more consistent and dedicated friend. I needed that life lesson, truth be told.

Every one of my new friends has created an enormous table for all to share. They have brought to that table a sense of purity, of reality, of love, and of a most charming existence. I wish that every one of them could see themselves the way I see them. Every person I have found here, it was not by accident. Every single moment counts here, and I am not about to look away and miss it. The Mediterranean is full of so much life, wonder, and magic. It brings you back into your body and makes you value your very special life. Maybe people live longer over here because no one ever wants to let it go. It's passion and paradise dressed up and disguised as really hard work.

Everything Has a Season

Everything has a season, from the foods and feasts to the wines and oils and also to you. Humans grow in season and change with every growing season. We have been many things under the sun throughout our years and we will continue to be many things more if we are so lucky. With each season that draws near, we grow and mature and turn into another version of ourselves. Those seasons are to be honored and appreciated much more than dreaded or avoided. It's hard to grow older. I'm feeling it too. I vacillate between missing my youth and loving my maturity. I am learning, especially here in Malta with all the seasonal foods and feasts, that everything has its day in the sun and any given thing doesn't stop having shining days just because it's no longer in season. Each season will come around again. We are all blooming in season and on time. Even if you can't yet see the fruits, trust that they will be ready when you are to come out and face the light.

Finding the Sweet Spot

What is the sweet spot of anything? It could be the dessert portion of your meal. It could be the time in your day when no one is pulling you in any direction and you can finally take a free breath and sit still. It could be the moment you see someone you love and the feelings that wash over you. That is definitely a sweet spot of any day! It could be the moment you get home and greet your beloved pet.

The sweet spot to me will probably mean something entirely different to you. It's your sweet spot that counts. Finding that sweet spot of the day, of the night, of the week, of the meal, whatever it is, it is yours to enjoy when it appears. It is also yours to notice. Oftentimes we fail to see that something so simple was actually one of our sweet-spot moments. Even in food, finding the sweet spot would generally imply finding that food when it is perfectly ripe and eating it right at that moment. That is surely a sweet-spot moment to savor! When I look at any plate of food, I take what I think would be the best bite or combination of the whole plate and set it to the side so I can have that bite last. I call it my perfect bite. That is a simple sweet-spot moment that I make sure to set up for pleasure no matter if it's a snack or a meal. It's something simple, but it brings me joy each and every time.

The countries along the Mediterranean grow the majority of their own food and eat according to the seasons. For example, when the berries are out of season, they vanish at the store until they are in season again. When certain foods come into season, everyone rushes to the local farm trucks or grocery stores to get them. When they make their debut in stores, the flavor is divine. In any large country, there is a multitude of produce available all year long, because it is imported from all over the world. However, the flavors are often muted by comparison.

In order to get something like bananas to a place far from where they are grown, they are cut when they are just getting green in hopes that they will turn yellow over the time it takes to transport them to another location. The maturing of such foods does not happen under the sun or in their natural habitat. The bananas do not get to hang from the tree until they're ready to be picked and eaten. It's why people who grew up in a place where banana trees are grown talk about how different the bananas they grew up with taste versus the bananas they find in parts of the world not near their original location.

There is nothing like pulling any food right off the vine or branch at exactly the time that it is perfectly ripe. Another example is the oranges growing outside my house. They have been green all summer, and I question whether they are ever going to turn orange. Now that it is the winter season, those oranges have quickly turned orange. And funnily enough, depending on the tree's orientation toward the sun, the oranges from some of my trees are super ripe and the juice we are making is sweet and sensational (hello, mimosas!), while at the same time the oranges on the trees growing on the side of my house facing a wall are not even fully orange yet. Their season is slightly behind the trees facing the front, where the sun can shine directly on them.

There is nothing wrong with the fact that some trees are ripe and ready to go, while other trees of the same planting and harvesting are not yet ready to ripen. They all end up having a perfectly ripe state when the time is right for them. It's our job to notice it and pull them at their peak time. It is simply an observation that the sun shines and brings them into the light at just the right time for each tree. One of the farmers told me that the farmers stick to one saying: "Let it ripen." Do not pull it early, but rather allow it to come into its own still hanging on the tree or bush before you pull it.

People who are local to where food is grown have a deeper level of appreciation and understanding about the way the natural world works through food and seem to be more comfortable with the parallels of natural life phases. We can learn a lot about following the seasons of our own lives by honoring how we feel and where we are as each season comes and goes. Growing old is a privilege denied to many. Do the best you can to handle it with grace and poise. It's okay to age, and you don't have to pretend to be young your entire life. Finding your sweet spot does not happen at only one certain age or stage. You will have plenty of sweet-spot moments to enjoy! Think of a sweet spot as a high time when the ebb and flow is in your favor. Notice when you are up there and relish it.

Sensitive Strawberries

Strawberries are what I consider the fruit equivalent of the super-sensitive human. Strawberries are very fragile and delicate and extremely susceptible to outside influences. Too much wind or rain and the strawberry fields will be wiped out before they begin. If a strawberry is sprayed with pesticides, it will absorb the poison more than will any other fruit or vegetable. Tending to strawberries is a daily to weekly affair and requires quite a lot of maintenance to ensure they are growing properly and will yield a bountiful harvest. Strawberries require a plastic covering to keep them from making direct contact with the soil. See? Sensitive!

There are many ways to grow strawberries according to where you are in the world and what you have available. But here in Malta, the strawberry fields are layered with a plastic coating to ensure that the strawberries grown in massive quantities are not compromised in any way. Strawberries don't come with an internal system that can differentiate between beneficial sprays and toxic sprays, and they take it all in no matter who or what they are around, including the sun, pollutants, debris from the winds, and whatever they are sprayed with by the growers. The soil is also sprayed here with a nontoxic spray to keep the red spiders away from the strawberries. If those spiders make it to the fruit, the strawberries will be destroyed. The farmers must handle the strawberries with great care from the very moment of planting to the time they come into full harvest.

The farmers know exactly what needs to be done to help the strawberries grow. Strawberries are one of the most demanding fruits on the block and require daily checking but with minimal handling as they mature. They require a close watch and a gentle hand every step of the way. If they are handled properly and protected well, they will turn into the most beautiful, bright, sweet-like-candy treats, packed with power. Strawberries have to be supported in their growth and celebrated when they finally make their debut. They go through such a series of colors, from almost white to lime green and finally to the beautiful red we know them for, the most perfect shade of red in the natural world. It's a transition to become so beautiful, and one that is hard-earned. But when they finally make their way out, the whole country celebrates.

This makes me think of young people as they go through adolescence and require a great deal of attention and watching but also need to be handled with minimum outright interference. There is an analogy that says children are like dogs when they are young, when they stick tight to their parents' side. Then they grow to be teenagers and become cats. They choose when they want to be around you and they sleep a great deal of the day.

Adolescence is a time of great sensitivity and change, and each person requires a very specific amount of time to mature. Even if all the strawberries are planted on the exact same day, they do not all become ripe at the same time. Everyone takes their time to get to the next phase, and these little gems are a great example of that in action. Strawberries also go through several months of needing daily care and constant watch (like a child), but a knowledge of when to step back and let them develop on their own is also required (like a sleepy teen). They go through so many phases of transition as they grow and mature into their adult selves when they are ready to be picked and eaten. Whether it's a strawberry or a person, that maturity, when it finally happens, is something to honor and celebrate.

Your Sensitive Superpower

Being sensitive is a superpower that many people try to dismiss as a weakness. It is one of the strongest attributes a person can carry and especially maintain. To find out if you are super sensitive or empathic, answer these questions and see how many ring true for you:

- Do you feel other people's emotions even if they don't tell you about them?
- Do you feel others' pain as if it were your own?
- Is it difficult for you to let go of situations that were not positive?
- Do you replay situations or words that people said over and over again?
- Do you feel that you are more aware of your surroundings than most?
- Do you feel that you are more sensitive to outside influences than others around you?
- Do you trust your gut?

If you answered yes to the first six of these questions, then I sincerely hope and pray that you answered yes to the last one. Your gut is your very best and most accurate guide. Always trust your instincts and the bodily sensations you get when you tap into outside influences that are dangerous, off-putting, or nerve-wracking or make you pause or that make you feel happy, at home, peaceful, and trusting even if it's someone new in your life. Trust that too. Your body is always your best indicator of information. Trust your gut always.

Festa Frawli

The festival that the whole country comes together to celebrate for the great strawberry harvest is known as Festa Frawli.[39] Celebrations in Malta are not just to honor the saints! This festival is only one day a year, and everyone drops what they are doing to get to it. There is not an exact date and not even an exact month anymore to this particular festival each year, as it is held according to the weather and the season. Even the locals know what a treasure it is to finally have the great strawberry achieve its metamorphosis and come out to play with the world around them!

With climate change (which is in no way up for debate here, but instead accepted and realized that it is real and has changed up all of the fruit and vegetable seasons), the date of the festival now changes according to when the year's strawberries are fully ripe and in season. The festival can be held anywhere between March and May, depending on the year's storms and sunlight. Once it has been determined when the strawberries will fully come into season, the farmers of the town notify the local council. From there, the local council and the head church at the square host the festival. They come together to put on quite the yearly event! Even the local schools in that town have the children draw pictures of strawberries and their artwork is hung throughout the town square.

Just a few strawberry items that are sold at the festival include strawberry buns, donuts, ice cream and sorbet, cheesecakes, muffins, pastries, and even strawberry cream-filled cannoli. Drinks include smoothies, liqueurs, strawberry lemonade, strawberry sangria…The list goes on and on. It is strawberry everything! Of course there is a live band outside playing music and the festival goes from morning until evening. There are alcoholic and nonalcoholic strawberry drinks that people can enjoy while they walk from table to table tasting and buying the many strawberry products. I highly suggest looking up "Strawberry Festa Frawli

---

39. European School of English (ESE), "Strawberry Fields Forever…The Festa Frawli Is Back!"

Malta" to see how massive this festival is. It is something that the locals look forward to every year.

Food for Thought: The Simplest Question

This little snack break offers the simplest questions of all:

- When was the last time you celebrated anything for yourself?
- How do you celebrate your life?
- How do you celebrate the ones you love?
- Do you celebrate your own life as much as other people's lives?

Are you someone who goes above and beyond for other people but seldom for yourself? Learn to celebrate you and your precious life in whatever ways make you feel special, supported, and loved. You are the one you have to live with. You are the constant denominator of your life, so you'd best get used to enjoying your own company. It's great to be a nice neighbor and a wonderful friend, but you must always include yourself among those you love most. If it's been a while since you celebrated something fun and wonderful, then maybe do it this week and let that party be all about you!

Food Tip and Recipe

Because of the many months of heat in Malta, ice cream and gelato are always in demand. Wherever you go in any town, you will find a gelato shop filled with the creamiest and most indulgent flavors. If you don't live in a place where gelato is served, you can always use ice cream or frozen yogurt in place of any part of these simple recipes.

Dark Chocolate Gelato with Sea Salt and Olive Oil (Recipe by Salvatore Romano)

Here is a true Italian recipe from the finest olive oil maker in all the land! This dessert recipe is from Salvatore Romano from Tasting Sicily as well as the Mediterranean Olive Oil Academy.

It's easier to buy gelato or ice cream than to make it from scratch, so I will present the recipe that way. Dark chocolate is ideal for this recipe.

DIRECTIONS

Sprinkle one scoop of dark chocolate ice cream or gelato with sea salt, then drizzle with olive oil. (The Bidni olive oil, if you can get it, might be a bold choice to bring out the sweet and spicy flavors.)

Frozen Greek Yogurt Sorbet with Watermelon (Recipe by Paul Parker)

INGREDIENTS

2 cups (300 grams) seedless watermelon, diced
3 cups (735 grams) plain full-fat Greek yogurt
½ cup (65 grams) dried cranberries

DIRECTIONS

In a blender, mix the watermelon and yogurt. Add the dried cranberries and stir. Put in the freezer for 4–6 hours, then separate into containers or glasses.

Toppings of choice are a chocolate-covered strawberry with sea salt and olive oil drizzle or pecans with a local honey drizzle.

TOPPINGS

To make either of the above desserts pop, add a chocolate-covered strawberry with sea salt and olive oil drizzle before serving, or add pecans with a local honey drizzle. The blend of savory, sweet, and salty is perfection.

Chocolate-Covered Strawberries with Sea Salt (Recipe by Emily Francis)

Whether it's the black chocolate base with sea salt and olive oil or the frozen yogurt base with fruit and sea salt and olive oil, it only gets better when you put a chocolate-covered strawberry on top and sprinkle the sea salt into the chocolate around the strawberry and then finish with the spicy Bidni olive oil or any high-quality olive oil to make it more decadent.

INGREDIENTS
High-quality baking chocolate
Fresh strawberries

DIRECTIONS
Melt the chocolate either in the microwave or using a double boiler. Melt most of the chocolate and then add a couple pieces of unmelted chocolate to reduce the temperature of the chocolate mix. Stir until creamy.

The strawberries should be rinsed off and dried. Dip the strawberries into the melted chocolate and then lay them on a piece of parchment paper until dry. Drizzle sea salt on top for added flair before the chocolate hardens.

Simply place the chocolate-covered strawberry on top of the gelato or frozen yogurt and then drizzle just a bit of olive oil on top to add an element of creamy, rich, oily texture to bring all the other flavors out. To give it that extra *oomph* and really make the flavors pop, you can always add some chopped almonds or pecans and drizzle with both olive oil and honey.

After-Meal Espresso and Digestif

"What is planted in each person's soul will sprout."
—Rumi

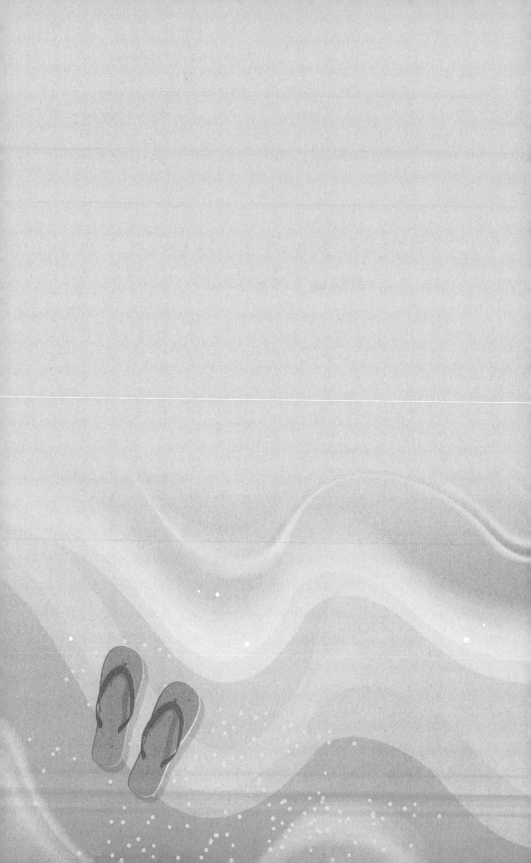

"It's Malta. It's Life."

This is your life! You keep what you like and leave the rest. There is a saying here in Malta when things are amazing and when things are horrible (which there is no shortage of in either direction, depending on what you are looking to find). They say as they shrug their shoulders, "Hey, it's Malta. What can you do? It's life. What can you do?" You are in it. You are not getting out alive, and you are not going back to when you were younger. You are as old as you've ever been and as young as you will ever get to be again. Don't dwell on a past version of yourself. Instead, work with what you've got and make it the best-tasting dish you've ever eaten. You are what you eat and you are still one very tasty dish!

What can you do to take life as it comes? Make it the best dish you could possibly prepare and then eat all of it, preferably with friends and loved ones. Like the Greeks that take the bread and drop it into the bottom of the salad bowl to soak up the flavors and olive oil that was left, it is a perfect metaphor for life. Soak it all up. Savor each and every bite and don't be afraid to get messy while you eat it. Every single tiny last crumb, eat it all. Feel and savor every ounce of joy that washes over you.

I've been saying it over and over throughout this book, but I will say it again to be sure it got through: If you are wishing to be someplace else in your life, I am begging you to permit yourself to go for it. You can always go back if it doesn't work out. But why not try? Why not give it everything you've got to create your very own delicious recipe for your life?

You deserve to live your very best life. There are no do-overs when you reach the finish line. It's now or it might be never.

You deserve to live the life of your dreams with the people you love the most, with the work you love to do, and with your physical, emotional, and spiritual environment supporting all of it in the location you most desire. There are people you haven't even met yet from all around the world just waiting to love you. If you are not happy, you have to be the one to change it. If you are quite content, then stay where you are, but give yourself permission to take it up a notch and live just a little bit more freely and maybe a little more fiercely, with a little more flavor. If you feel like you have everything you've ever wanted, then I encourage you to be willing to take a vacation and see more of the world just for your fun and enjoyment. It also makes you love your life and your home sweet home even more when you return!

Maybe you will decide from reading this book that you want to visit Malta and see where movies like *Troy* and *Popeye* and the first season of *Game of Thrones* were filmed in real life. We say, "Mela! And welcome!" Maybe you realize that the Mediterranean in all its magic and glory is something you'd like to learn more about, or maybe there is a particular food you'd like to study, like the olive oils that are grown all over this part of the world. Whatever got you excited from reading this book, follow those ideas and see where they lead.

What I find the most refreshing is that everything is just a little bit more relaxed on this side of the pond. People are not very interested in what's happening in your life unless you invite them into it. Otherwise, they are perfectly happy not to bother with telling you what you do wrong as a person. Most likely, they have not even thought about what might be right or wrong with you. They are too involved in what is happening in their own lives to be bothered by such things. They will be more than happy to offer suggestions on what to order or what to make and how to make it when it comes to foods, drinks, and celebrations! Those are all fair game here, and if you are like me, you will listen up and learn from their suggestions!

After-Meal Espresso

After however many courses you may eat in one sitting, you will always be offered an after-meal espresso. You can have your espresso with dessert or following dessert or in place of any dessert. It's up to you. As they say here so often, "As you wish." Espresso is small, it fits the flavor profile of a true coffee lover, it allows people to sit together long after the meal is finished, and it is a wonderful aid. It warms the body and is a great exclamation point at the end of the meal experience.

When I go out with my girlfriends to enjoy time together, we often eat at one restaurant and then leave that place for our after-meal espresso at another location. That allows us to walk around a bit and take in the fresh air before sitting down again at the next stop. Usually the wine will be had with the meal at the first restaurant and the espresso will be for another place. It seems to have the effect of prolonging a night of fun and friendship. That little tiny cup of super strong coffee allows for a new atmosphere and more conversation to occur.

Here is another little secret of the Mediterranean: drinking coffee after a meal speeds up the digestion process by stimulating the muscles of the intestinal tract. Drinking coffee following a meal helps to move food out of the body more quickly.[40] The health and social benefits to that after-meal coffee or espresso serve to improve the social experience, the dining experience, and the overall quality of our lives.

In each country, they have very different methods of drinking their after-meal espresso. The one thing they have in common is that no matter how you take your coffee, making it with the highest-quality beans is something all Mediterraneans take quite seriously. Some only drink the coffee standing up, while others like to sit down and relax with it. Some add spices, alcohol, or sweets to the coffee, while others like it black and strong. Honestly, there are too many details to dive into, but suffice it to say that every culture does it in its own distinct and unique way. Coffee

---

40. Dryden, "How Drinking Coffee after a Meal Can Help You Lose Weight," and Carta Coffee Merchants, "Why Do People Drink Coffee after Dinner?"

itself is the common practice following a meal, and whatever way you choose to take your coffee is up to you…*as you wish.*

After-Meal *Digestif*

To top off the full experience with the *apéritif,* the appetizers, the main courses, the desserts, and the after-dinner espresso, there is one more little hidden gem to offer you. You guessed it: it's the *digestif* shot. This can be bourbon, brandy, port, or the Mediterranean specialty: limoncello.

Believe it or not, once you have enjoyed a *digestif* following your coffee, you can get back to drinking wine (or any alcoholic beverage) or call it a night. The *digestif* seems to be the shot that brings your body back into drinking alcohol again following the meal should you wish to or marks a solid ending to a fine dining experience. These people are true party animals! To be fair, the meal is spread out over many hours to enjoy together. With everything they do here, there is always a method to their madness. It is all in support of the natural flow within the body, both in food and in life. The sea, the culture, the food and drink…it all teaches us how to go with the flow and not against it. I have learned to let go of trying to hold on so tight and steer every outcome. If you let go a little bit and try to taste the joys, life can surely surprise you!

Saħħa: Goodbye and Good Health

When we raise a glass and give a toast in Malta, we say *saħħa,* which means "to health!" We say it when we clink our glasses and also when we wave goodbye. But before we go and say saħħa, I want to ask you one thing: What would you do if you looked around and realized that there is no place else in the entire world you would rather be than exactly where you are now? I ask that concerning your location, your vocation, your friends, your family, and above all within yourself. I have found my soul here in Malta. My senses of happy, joy, and bliss have been waiting for me to come and find them and soak them up. My joy lives and thrives in the Mediterranean. I finally feel like I am blooming in season and on time.

I invite you to join me in seeking out a sacred sense of happiness, joy, and bliss in allowing yourself the freedom to find everything you are looking for in your life and make it the most delicious dish you have ever eaten. Don't doubt for a single minute that you do not deserve to live the life of your dreams. Where you are matters. What it took for you to get there matters even more. Who you are becoming is important. The lessons you take with you are valuable. Trust the process and your growth. Trust the seasons and each of the blossoms as they unfold. You have everything it takes to make your wildest dreams bloom into reality.

Your JOY is waiting for you to take a bite!

Food for Thought: Take It All In

This is your wonderful, beautiful, amazing life! Do not waste it! Look around you and find the magic and mystery that lives everywhere around you. If you don't see it where you are right this moment, all you need to do is open a window or take a walk outside to find the beauty. Twirl yourself around in a 360-degree turn and notice the true beauty of your surroundings, then find a place right in the middle of it to sit down and be still.

Close your eyes and exhale fully before you begin. Empty your lungs and empty your mind of any cluttering thoughts. Now inhale a full but not too large breath and hold it for a moment. Do you feel it? It is purpose. It is the reminder that you are alive on this planet at exactly this time in history. Exhale and release any tension or heaviness that might be in your body or your thoughts.

With each slow and complete inhale, take in one simple word or thought that brings you closer to feelings of happiness, joy, or bliss. With each exhale, release one word or thought that takes you away from happiness, joy, or bliss. Continue with this practice until you get to one solid inhale and exhale, sharing the same single word in and the same single word out.

For example, you may start with a lot of different words on your inhale and exhale, but as you go along and stay true to the practice, you will find that the outside words fall away and the main meal of words remains.

Here is an example:

Inhale *peace.*   Exhale *destruction.*

Inhale *calm.*   Exhale *distraction.*

Inhale *happy.*   Exhale *sadness.*

Inhale *joy.*   Exhale *despair.*

Inhale *bliss.*   Exhale *frustration.*

Inhale *love.*   Exhale *fear.*

Inhale *love.*   Exhale *fear.*

Inhale *love.*   Exhale *fear.*

By the end, you will focus deeply on one repetitive word (in this case *love*) that brings you peace and happiness. You will exhale and release one concept (such as *fear*) that helps you let go of everything else. Focus on those words and on your breath as the words make themselves known to you. They will deepen your awareness of what you really want and also what you don't want. This practice helps you identify what to let go of and what brings you closer to feelings of joyful peace. Let those simple words lead you into a place where you are fully aware of how precious your life really is.

Remember, you are the only you in the whole wide world. There is no one else exactly like you. What you bring to the table is a magic all your own. It cannot be duplicated or replaced. Do everything you can to appreciate the life you have been given and take those extra steps to make it the best meal you've ever experienced. Like a fine wine, you are only getting better with age.

Sahha!

When Life Hands You Lemons in the Mediterranean, You Make Limoncello

Limoncello is a very common *digestif* in the Mediterranean. It is originally from the Amalfi Coast and the island of Capri. This is a recipe from my own family on the Italian side. They still live in Northern Italy. The recipe was handed down to me by my great-uncle, who got it from a grandmother from the island of Capri.

Limoncello
(Recipe by Fabrizio Oliva)

All along the Mediterranean, limoncello is a well-known and well-loved drink. Serve it chilled in small shot glasses. If you can't find real Capri lemons, be sure to use organically grown lemons without pesticides.

INGREDIENTS

1 liter food alcohol, about 95% proof (Vodka is most commonly used.)
10–12 Capri lemons (10 if large, 12 if small)
750 grams (3¼ cups) sugar
1.5 liters (6¼ cups) water

METHOD

Of the lemon, only the yellow part of the peel is used. The white part makes it bitter, so use a potato peeler to remove this part, being careful not to break the microcapsules of the peel that contain the essential oil.

Peel the lemons and put the yellow parts of the peel and the alcohol in a glass container for at least 10–15 days. Shake once a day without opening.

After 15 days, prepare the syrup separately by boiling the water and sugar. Then let it cool down.

When the syrup is cold (about 2 liters), filter the alcohol. The lemon peels are thrown away, and the alcohol that has now turned yellow is added to the syrup.

The recipe will yield about 3 liters of limoncello with an alcohol content of about 32–33%.

Leave to rest in the refrigerator for at least a week, then put in the freezer. Always serve cold. Limoncello is a good digestive.

"It always seems impossible until it's done."
—Commonly attributed to Nelson Mandela

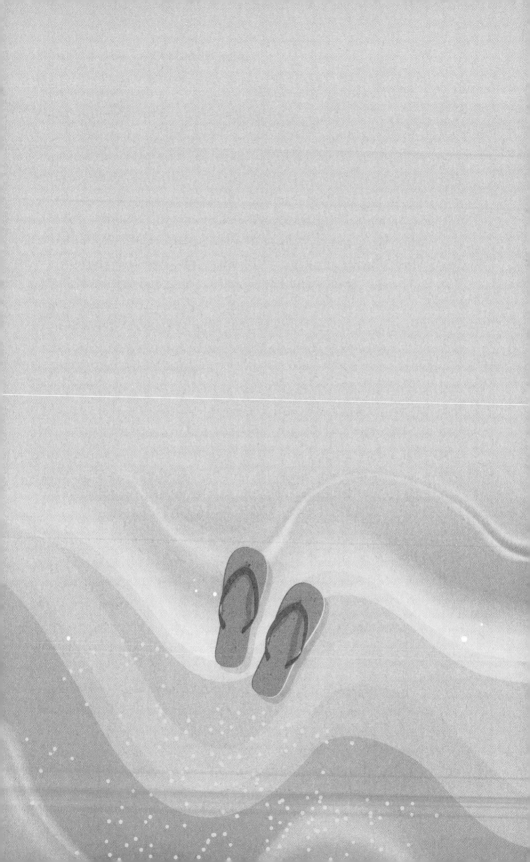

References

Angelou, Maya. *I Know Why the Caged Bird Sings.* New York: Random House, 1969.

Aperol. "Aperol Spritz Ritual." Accessed August 2022. https://www.aperol.com/en-us/product/aperol-spritz-ritual/.

Ascher, Michael. "The Opposite of Addiction Is Not Sobriety—It Is Human Connection." Michael Ascher, M.D. Accessed August 20222. https://aschermd.com/the-opposite-of-addiction-is-not-sobriety-it-is-human-connection/.

Beck, Madalyn. "Start Over, My Darling Backstory." *Madalyn Beck* (blog). Feb. 27, 2020. https://www.madalynbeck.com/start-over-my-darling/.

Brown, Maressa. "Astrocartography Is the Key to Planning Dream Vacations and Making Fulfilling Moves." InStyle. December 30, 2021. https://www.instyle.com/lifestyle/astrology/astrocartography.

Campbell, Joseph. *The Power of Myth.* New York: Anchor Books, 1991.

Carta Coffee Merchants. "Why Do People Drink Coffee after Dinner?" October 5, 2017. https://www.cartacoffee.com/blogs/island-blog/why-do-people-drink-coffee-after-dinner.

Chevalier, Gaétan, Stephen Sinatra, James Oschman, Karol Sokal, and Pawel Sokal. "Earthing: Health Implications of Reconnecting the Human Body to the Earth's Surface Electrons." *Journal of Environmental and Public Health* (January 12, 2012): 291541. https://pubmed.ncbi.nlm.nih.gov/22291721/.

Christianity.com. "What Is the Tree of Life? Bible Meaning and Importance." October 21, 2021. https://www.christianity.com/wiki/christian-terms/tree-of-life-bible-meaning.html.

The Cliffs Interpretation Centre. "The Oldest Cultivated Mediterranean Fruit Species: Figs." October 6, 2020. https://www.thecliffs.com.mt/the-oldest-cultivated-mediterranean-fruit-species-figs-10062020/.

Cooper Hewitt, Smithsonian Design Museum. "Malta." Accessed August 2022. https://collection.cooperhewitt.org/countries/23424897.

Danton, Tim. "What Do Bill Gates, Steve Jobs and Scott McNealy Have in Common? They're Lucky." Alphr. July 1, 2009. https://www.alphr.com/bill-gates/33541/what-do-bill-gates-steve-jobs-and-scott-mcnealy-have-in-common-they-re-lucky.

Dooley, Mike. *Manifesting Change*. New York: Atria Books, 2010.

Doyle, Glennon. *Carry On, Warrior*. New York: Scribner, 2014.

Dr. Oz Show. "Organic Grocery List: Potatoes." Accessed August 2022. https://www.drozshow.com/slideshow/organic-grocery-list/potatoes.

Drury, Melanie. "Tears of Blood! Here Are Some of Malta's Most Famous 'Miracles.'" GuideMeMalta.com. May 5, 2019. https://www.guidememalta.com/en/tears-of-blood-here-are-some-of-malta-s-most-famous-miracles.

Dryden, Fiona. "How Drinking Coffee after a Meal Can Help You Lose Weight." DerbyshireLive. April 23, 2018. https://www.derbytelegraph.co.uk/news/uk-world-news/weight-loss-coffee-metabolism-diet-1490923.

Emily in Malta. "Emily in Malta: Gozitan Sea Salt." Oh My Malta, September 17, 2021. https://ohmymalta.com.mt/2021/09/17/emily-in-malta-gozitan-sea-salt/.

Encyclopædia Britannica. "Bollywood: Film Industry, India." Accessed August 2022. https://www.britannica.com/topic/Bollywood-film-industry-India.

EricT_CulinaryLore. "Spilling Salt Is Bad Luck and Other Salt Superstitions." Culinary Lore. March 24, 2014. https://culinarylore.com/food-myths:spilling-salt-is-bad-luck-and-more/.

European School of English (ESE). "Strawberry Fields Forever… The Festa Frawli Is Back!" April 4, 2022. https://ese-edu.com/2022/04/04 /festa-frawli-2022/.

Fava, Jean Pierre. "The Miraculous Story of the Maltese Lady of the Grotto." Aleteia. September 8, 2020. https://aleteia.org/2020/09/08 /the-miraculous-story-of-the-maltese-lady-of-the-grotto/.

———. "The Miraculous Story of Our Lady of Ta' Pinu National Shrine, in Gozo." Aleteia. August 15, 2020. https://aleteia.org/2020/08/15 /the-miraculous-story-of-our-lady-of-ta-pinu-national-shrine-in-gozo/.

Gladwell, Malcom. *Outliers: The Story of Success.* New York: Hachette, 2011.

Grapes and Figs Ministry. "The Fig Tree: What the Bible Says about Figs." Faithlife. Accessed August 2022. https://faithlife.com/gafm /newsletters/21481879.

Hari, Johann. "Johann Hari." TED. Accessed August 2022. https://www .ted.com/speakers/johann_hari.

Hedley-Dent, Ticky. "So Why Do We Throw Salt over Our Shoulder? Answers to the Strangest Superstitions." Daily Mail. Updated May 10, 2011. https://www.dailymail.co.uk/femail/article-1385380/Why-throw -salt-shoulder-superstitions-answered.html.

Ians. "The Enigmatic Indian Film Industry & Its Expansive Reach." The Hans India. August 3, 2022. https://www.thehansindia.com /hans/opinion/news-analysis/the-enigmatic-indian-film-industry -its-expansive-reach-756146.

Interesting Engineering. "Mysterious Ancient Temples Resonate at the 'Holy Frequency.'" December 1, 2016. https://interestingengineering .com/science/temples-resonates-frequency-111-hz.

Jackson, Cindy. "A Basket of Figs." *Times of Malta.* July 16, 2011. https: //timesofmalta.com/articles/view/A-basket-of-figs.376162.

Koliós S.A. Greek Dairy. "Authentic Greek Yogurt 10% Fat." Accessed August 2022. https://www.kolios.gr/en/our_products/authentic -greek-yogurt-range/authentic-greek-yogurt-10/.

Leonard, Jayne. "Does Pink Himalayan Salt Have Any Health Benefits?" Medical News Today. July 30, 2018. https://www.medicalnewstoday.com/articles/315081.

Magri, Giulia. "Maltese Ftira Added to UNESCO's Intangible Cultural Heritage List." Times of Malta. December 16, 2020. https://timesof malta.com/articles/view/maltese-ftira-added-to-unescos-intangible -cultural-heritage-list.839294.

Malin, Sheryl and Dan. "Follow Your Bliss and the Universe Will Open Doors Where There Were Only Walls." *The Journey to Good Health* (blog). February 27, 2022. https://www.thejourneytogoodhealth.com /single-post/follow-your-bliss-and-the-universe-will-open-doors -where-there-were-only-walls.

Mallia, Jillian. "A Real Life-Saver: Gozo's Ta' Pinu Is a Magnificent Church with an Incredible Story." GuideMeMalta.com. April 17, 2022. https://www.guidememalta.com/en/a-real-life-saver-gozo -s-ta-pinu-is-a-magnificent-church-with-an-incredible-story.

Malta Independent. "2,000-Year-Old Trees Still Producing Olives." August 16, 2011. https://www.independent.com.mt/articles/2011 -08-16/news/2000-year-old-trees-still-producing-olives-297296.

Malta.com. "Feast of St. Gregory in Zejtun." Accessed August 2022. https://www.malta.com/en/coverage/2012/feast-of-saint-gregory -celebrated-in-malta-0044.

McKenna, Stacey. "Malta's Hypogeum, One of the World's Best Preserved Prehistoric Sites, Reopens to the Public." Smithsonian Magazine. May 23, 2017. https://www.smithsonianmag.com/travel/maltas -hypogeum-one-worlds-best-preserved-prehistoric-sites-reopen s-public-180963397/.

National Records of Scotland. "Hairy Thyme." Accessed August 2022. https://www.nrscotland.gov.uk/research/archivists-garden/index-by -plant-name/hairy-thyme.

Nutritionix. "Greek Yogurt, Berries & Cream: Dannon Light & Fit: Nutrition Facts." Updated September 14, 2021. https://www

.nutritionix.com/i/dannon-light-fit/greek-yogurt-berries-cream
/5c1c99ae7a7848a3182c3de5.

One for Israel. "The Symbolism of Figs in the Bible." June 2, 2016.
https://www.oneforisrael.org/bible-based-teaching-from-israel/figs
-in-the-bible/.

Pisani, Daniel. *A Plant Based Maltese Kitchen.* Malta: Daniel Pisani, 2021.

The Salt Box. "Dead Sea Salt: The Ultimate Guide to Uses, Origins,
Benefits." May 21, 2020. https://www.thesaltbox.com.au/news/dead
-sea-salt-the-ultimate-guide-to-uses-origins-benefits/.

Siegel, Bernie S. *Love, Medicine & Miracles.* New York: HarperPerennial,
1998.

Suzy. "Avgolemono Soup Recipe (Greek Lemon Chicken Soup)." The
Mediterranean Dish. Modified November 10, 2020. https://www
.themediterraneandish.com/avgolemono-soup-recipe/.

Team Leverage Edu. "Top Rumi Quotes to Celebrate Love, Life, Nature,
Sufism & the Universe!" Leverage Edu. Updated on October 22, 2021.
https://leverageedu.com/blog/rumi-quotes/.

Times of Malta. "Sneaking a Peak behind the Prison Walls." November 5,
2013. https://timesofmalta.com/articles/view/Sneaking-a-peak
-behind-the-prison-walls.493551.

Visit Malta. "Village Festas." Accessed August 2022. https://www.visit
malta.com/en/a/village-festas/.

A Wandering Medic. "Ta' Pinu National Shrine: An Architectural
Masterpiece." Accessed August 2022. https://awanderingmedic.com
/ta-pinu-national-shrine/.

Wheeler, Philip. "The Unique Relationship Between the Fig and the Fig
Wasp." OpenLearn. Updated November 4, 2020. https://www.open
.edu/openlearn/nature-environment/natural-history/the-unique
-relationship-between-the-fig-and-the-fig-wasp

Xuereb, Justin. "Restaurants on the Edge by Netflix." Xwejni Salt Pans by
Leli tal-Melh. June 17, 2020. https://xwejnisaltpans.com/blogs/news
/restaurants-on-the-edge-by-netflix.

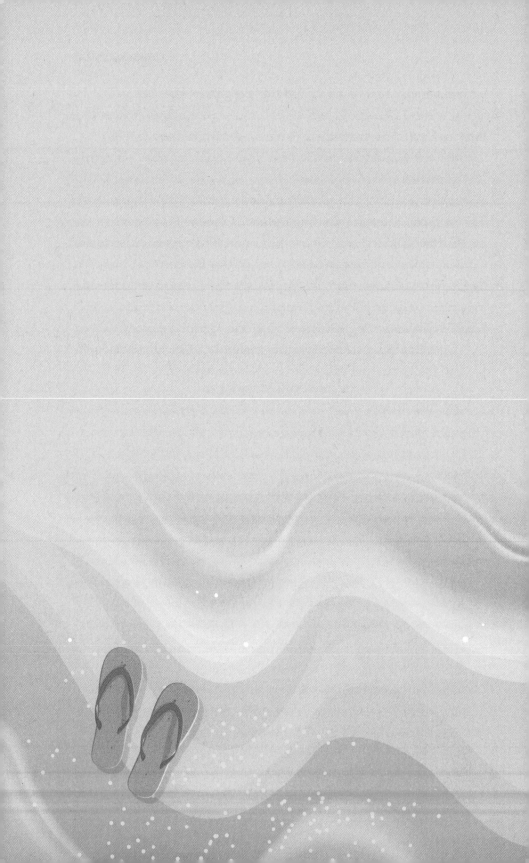

To Write to the Author

If you wish to contact the author or would like more information about this book, please write to the author in care of Llewellyn Worldwide Ltd. and we will forward your request. Both the author and the publisher appreciate hearing from you and learning of your enjoyment of this book and how it has helped you. Llewellyn Worldwide Ltd. cannot guarantee that every letter written to the author can be answered, but all will be forwarded. Please write to:

Emily A. Francis
℅ Llewellyn Worldwide
2143 Wooddale Drive
Woodbury, MN 55125-2989
Please enclose a self-addressed stamped envelope for reply,
or $1.00 to cover costs. If outside the U.S.A., enclose
an international postal reply coupon.

Many of Llewellyn's authors have websites with additional information and resources. For more information, please visit our website at http://www.llewellyn.com.

Notes

Notes

Notes

Notes

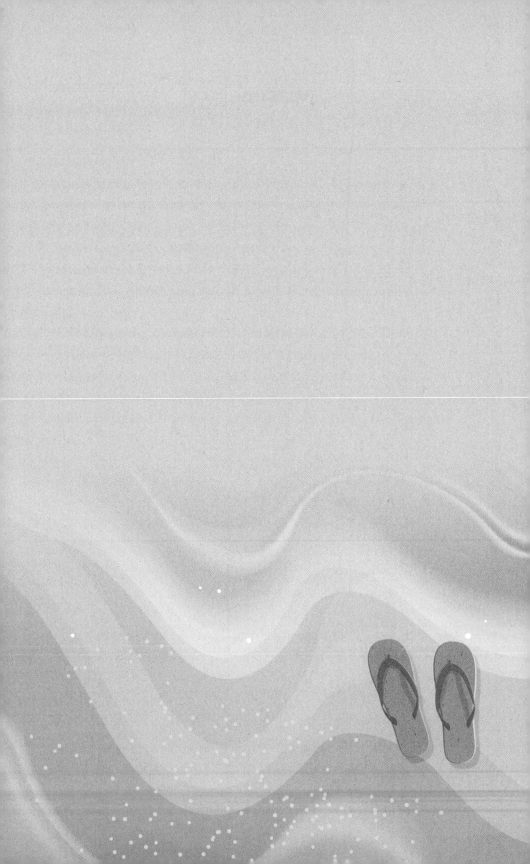